Five Ways To Focus

Focus

JULIA WOLFENDALE

This work was first published in the
United Kingdom in November 2021,
as an e-book by On The Up Books
ontheupconsulting.com

British Library Cataloguing in
Publication Data available.

Paperback ISBN: 978-1-8381583-2-3

E-book ISBN: 978-1-8381583-3-0

Client Testimonials

'Julia helped me journey towards being a better version of myself. Nothing more could be asked of a coach.'

'Julia gave me the tools to think reflectively and consider what is it that I want, rather than what I feel is expected of me, which gave me a lot more confidence moving forward.'

'First Chief Executive roles are daunting. Julia made a big difference in the development of my positive mindset and gave me a confidence I needed to be effective and impactful in my role.'

To my wonderful husband Al, who always
knows what matters.

FIVE WAYS TO FOCUS

'During my coaching sessions with Julia her approach regularly resulted in me experiencing 'lightbulb' moments and I always came away with focus and clarity on what was important to me and my development as a senior leader. This has been invaluable in both my professional and personal life.'

'Coaching with Julia has crystallised my purpose and what is important to me. We've explored ways to manage overwhelm and make times for the things that really matter. I now have the confidence to continue to take practical steps towards my goals and to let go of things that are holding me back. I now believe my dream is possible and that I can make it a reality. I've experienced a shift to a more positive perspective. I've made practical, tangible changes.'

'Julia is skilled at cutting through the noise and enabling you to clearly focus on the issues. I always feel energised and focused after our sessions. My coaching sessions with Julia really make a difference and it's time well spent. Often challenging but always supportive, I have grown so much during our time together.'

'Our senior management team now have a quote, 'what would Julia say?!' This does several things. Firstly, it makes us laugh & brings us back together again. Secondly, it makes us reflect on what we have just said, noticing the impact, positive or negative on colleagues and thirdly it helps us communicate!

Contents

'Successful people maintain a positive focus in life no matter what is going on around them. They stay focused on their past successes rather than their past failures and on the next action steps they need to take to get them closer to the fulfilment of their goals rather than all the other distractions that life presents to them.'

Jack Canfield

Preface

Too much to do, not enough hours in the day, week, month, and then before you know it you are asking yourself, 'where did the time go?' and 'why have I not accomplished what matters to me?'

Perhaps we shouldn't take life too seriously as no one gets out alive. But surely it is worth giving it our best shot. Life can sometimes seem like a constant game of Whack-A-Mole. Just when you deal with one thing another thing sprouts up that demands your attention, interrupts your plan (or your plan to make a plan), pierces your precious peace, and creates fury and frustration.

When we feel the odds are stacked against us and overwhelm envelops us, it could be a sign it is time to shizazzle things up a little. This book will help you stop making mountains out of molehills and focus just on what counts, giving you chance to draw breath, boost your brain power with renewed headspace, and get perspective so you can enjoy what life has to offer you and get things on the up!

> *'...the natural process of disorientation*
> *and reorientation that marks*
> *the turning points in the path of*
> *growth,' William Bridges*

The important thing is to notice what brings you here and believe that the future can be bright. Your choices from this point onwards can put you on a path of positivity where life feels fulfilling rather than overfilled.

Change Points and Boiling Points

You may find yourself at a **change point**, experiencing a life change; that may include a shift in your important relationships, family situation, health, or work-life priorities. These transitions can leave us discombobulated, unsure of how to process the new thoughts and feelings that arise. Or you may be approaching a milestone birthday and find yourself morbidly measuring what remains of your own mortality.

Or perhaps you sense you are at a **boiling point** knowing that something is not working for you. The pressure is building, and you know you need to find a way to dial down the heat and give yourself a way to discover what you can do to love your life more. Five Ways to Focus is an approach that will help you to reorient yourself towards what matters.

In my own career I have noticed when I was at a change point myself and knew that if I didn't make a move, I would reach a boiling point. I am now doing work I love doing, with people I love working with and making a difference every day. There have been some tough times, but once I knew what mattered to me. the changes I made were completely right for me. It took courage, yes, but the starting point was to know what I wanted and take the first step towards that goal with a commitment to myself.

I will help you to cultivate a mindset of purposeful positivity, a readiness and enthusiasm for focusing on the good stuff. By inviting you to reflect on key coaching questions you will slow down your busy mind. You will cut through the cognitive clutter to gain the clarity, insight, and perspective you need to take positive action. I will check you are ready for the changes you are considering and encourage you to commit to what you truly can do and what you know will make a difference. The impact of understanding what is holding you back and what you can overcome could be very empowering for you. Taking ownership of your personal development is right at the heart of this book.

'Nurture your mind with great thoughts, for you will never go any higher than you think.'- Benjamin Disraeli

Cultivating a sense of clarity is key to getting things on the up. With a clear mind, you can create the space for new intentions to be formed, and new ideas to flourish. Planning for *and* making positive changes will help you to grow.

As a professional development coach, I love to inspire people to be their best selves by making the tough stuff easy to talk about and deal with. I coach people through difficult situations and transitions, supporting them to discover their talents and passions and the practical actions that can create a positive impact. With this book I can help you too.

I work with all sorts of people from CEOs and Directors and leaders in large organisations, who want to master the art of being their best selves, as well as young people on youth development programmes, who are ready to put disadvantage behind them and discover new opportunities.

Confidence, aspiration, and clarity can be borne from a compassionate curiosity and an insightful question. I know that when I ask questions people tap into their inner wisdom and let their true potential shine through. I have seen my clients 'light up' when they see a way forward beyond what is clouding their thinking and preventing their progress.

Here I will share my approach to help you explore what matters to you and understand what you are looking for so you can focus on that and feel happier, more fulfilled and achieve the success you seek.

Why Five Ways?

Five Ways to Focus began its life as a coaching tool that I designed for working directly with my clients. I soon realized that I was using the approach with increasing regularity and set about developing the Five Ways to Focus as a self-led coaching programme on the online learning platform Udemy.com udemy.com/course/five-ways-to-focus-a-self-led-coaching-programme. The programme has enabled people across the world to use simple prompts to deal with overwhelm and find greater focus and fulfilment.

When I use Five Ways to Focus with clients, the simple framework helps to clarify their thinking to plan practical action. There is science behind why this works as an approach - behavioural science, which we will explore together. The Five Ways to Focus® approach has formed part of an award-winning programme at the Training Journal Awards 2019. This book is the natural follow-on from the direct coaching work, training, and the online programme, that has helped many people, and this is what brings me now to you.

I am rooting for you.

It is time to focus. Let's do this together. Let us explore and answer the questions that will help

13

you live your best life, be more effective, happy, successful, and fulfilled. When you reach the final chapter, I hope that you will have become so attuned to finding ways to focus that you will have the clarity to deal with complexity and be able to move forwards with purpose and poise. Such is my hope for you.

Already I am picturing you floating serenely through life from one deeply fulfilling life experience to the next, feeling the joy and being your best self. I hope you enjoy Five Ways to Focus and the results it will bring.

1. Introduction

The Start

So, here you are right at the start of something new. This is an approach that might challenge you and might change you. Five Ways to Focus will help you to see what to cherish and nurture and what no longer serves you. Whether you are looking to make a significant change in your life, or if you just need to assess how things are going, and which areas need a boost, then this book is for you.

Of course, if you are already in the zen zone 100% of the time and have the inner peace of a Buddhist monk, then that is brilliant. Good for you! Now move along, tiptoe back to the temple. This is for the rest of us, the normal people that have real lives, jobs, families, responsibilities, fears and hopes, insecurities, and aspirations. It is for the great majority who are trying to make it in the world, or get through life, dealing with ambiguity to achieve ambitions, and trying to handle complexity and disappointments positively. Five Ways to Focus is for you if you are spinning more plates than you would see at a global clown convention, or have fingers in more pies than Sweeney Todd's Mrs Lovett. You are most welcome here.

Who This Book Is For

You might recognise that you are at a boiling point and need to focus your mind to take the mental heat off a difficult situation. Or alternatively, at a change point and focus is needed to make a shift towards something better. Or you might be seeking some tips and tricks that will help you next time the mental fog starts to gather, and you feel yourself slipping towards uncertainty or unhappiness.

Ultimately, this book is for people who are:

- Feeling overwhelmed.
- Sensing that they are stuck and frustrated with their personal or work situation.
- Having difficulty dealing with distraction.
- Want to know how to prioritise what really matters.
- Want to feel more positive.
- Want to take practical actions.
- Have a sense that things could be better but are unsure how to make that happen.
- Want to start living their best life.

- YOU!

The Fog

In truth, few of us have it all figured out, many of us are in a fog. We experience trials, tribulations, and transitions in the days, weeks, months and years of our lives. Sometimes we feel as though we are bumbling blindly through from one thing to the next, repeating behaviours that do not give us the results we desire. We are busy and distracted, we forget to take the moments to stop, reflect, refocus, refresh, and reset. You are not on your own with this. It is a modern-day paradox that whilst we are more 'connected' socially we have become less connected to who we are and what matters to us than ever before.

In our modern lives, we are often overwhelmed by information and choices, this excess of external stimuli is causing us to detach from the feelings and thoughts that are truly aligned to us being our best selves. We lose our innate ability to make good decisions when we rely heavily on social media to tell us what to worry about, what to wear, who to take notice of. We are losing our ability to connect and focus on ourselves as individuals.

The following chapters will help you discover the way you want to be, and how to be your best self, more of the time, more equipped to deal with life's changes and challenges. When you know what to focus on, you can learn how to minimize distractions and give attention to the things that will make a positive difference to you.

Once, you know what you
are drawn to and why you
can start to create and enjoy
the life you are intentional
about living.

Do Less, Get More Rewards

This book is not about organization and productivity or how to supercharge your powers of doing more in less time. Quite the opposite, you will see how to do less and get more rewards. I will help you focus on what is in front of you, to see what you want beyond that, to be clear on how to get to where you want to be.

By encouraging you to look at the things that do matter to you and ensure they get the attention they deserve, you will understand what drains your energy and your time. I will prompt you to decide what you will do more or less of. This will equip you to make plans to move forwards in the areas of your life that need more focus and positive attention.

A Life you Love

People are questioning what makes them happy and are looking for new ways to have a fulfilling life. The coronavirus pandemic brought about a change like no other when shops, restaurants, offices, airports, universities, nurseries, and schools were closed around the world for months. Social contact shrunk to immediate family circles and entertainment was eked out by bingeing on boxsets. The months of disarray, disruption, loss, fear, and uncertainty have challenged us to think differently about work and family, our homes, our health, and our social lives. For many of us, there is a great need to review our lives and refocus on what matters.

Life should not feel combative, it is not a battle. That is not to say that we should not expect to experience difficulties. As the psychologist, Susan David in her YouTube video '*The gift and power of emotional courage*' pointedly observes that if we aspire to have no worries or concerns, if we don't want to ever feel sad or frustrated or deal with other difficult emotions then "we have dead people's goals." Not an ideal strategy for winning at life, but more of a way to passively experience it unchallenged, unchanged, and unfulfilled.

It is part of the human condition as soulful creatures to feel, to emote; we need to find ways to handle these feelings better. Some of the toughest times are our best lessons should we choose to see them that way. When we are overwhelmed, it is hard to see a positive way forward. We need to know what to pay attention to.

Learning to Focus

When you know what to focus on, you can learn how to minimise the distractions, and make conscious choices to pay attention to what will make a real difference. Using the Five Ways to Focus© model gives you a chance to see what you think.

It helps you to develop a new perspective, by drawing attention to those things that have eluded you and become a blind spot whilst all the noise of the outside world has been wreaking its influence. Once you know what you are drawn to, and why, you can start to create the life you are intentional about living. You can plan the actions that align with your true nature, your purpose in the world, and which generate the rewards you seek. You can focus on what matters.

Of course, there will always be disruptions, that is life, and we need to reasonably expect them and be emotionally well enough with the headspace to deal with what presents itself to us. Naturally, we get caught up in the day-to-day, the minute-to-minute distractions. Often, we are only dealing with what comes up and not thinking about what really deserves our time and attention.

As we go through this book you will see that when distractions and disasters occur in life (as they undoubtedly will) you can apply your five ways to focus techniques. By the end of the book, you will have learned how to hone the skills in knowing what to focus on and have a true sense of what deserves and requires your attention. You will have discovered a way to be kinder to yourself and learned to enjoy the feeling of being more at ease with renewed clarity and peace of mind.

Why Five?

Five is both a suitably simple and highly functional number. We have five fingers on each hand and five toes on each foot which help us handle what we need to carry and keep us stable, grounded, well-balanced, and upright. So why not six or seven? Five is universally regarded as an easily quantifiable number of things we can all get our heads around.

You may be familiar with the worldwide public health campaign 'Five A Day' recommending at least five fruit and vegetable portions per day as a part of a healthy diet to prevent cancer and heart disease. When it was launched, nutritionists around the world (who, obviously love their vegetables) argued for at least seven helpings. But the social scientists won that food fight in maintaining that, for optimal behavioural change and the required shift in people's diets, five was both an achievable and palatable amount for the majority.

Simplicity Equals Success

Five works, as we can easily see and hold five things in our minds without being overwhelmed. (I know, your head is full already most of the time!) People can engage with a small number of changes easily, by keeping track and holding themselves to account - key components for any behavioural change initiative. Any more than five is perhaps too much, any less and the impacts and benefits are reduced.

Simplicity equals success, memorable messages help people make changes that stick. So, your Five Ways to Focus will be a framework to:

- look at life afresh,
- develop a healthy and helpful perspective

- be ready to make the changes to achieve what matters most to you.

The Realm of Overwhelm

Ok, so sometimes you are overwhelmed and unclear on what to do. You struggle to commit to plans and have difficulty focusing your time and attention on things you know are important to you. Well, please do not be too hard on yourself because it is not surprising really.

We live in a time of the 'always on' culture. We go through our days in a constant state of distraction. Just because everyone else is doing it too, does not mean it is ok for you and you might be sensing the negative effects of this in your own personal and professional life right now. When bad habits become the norm in our social or professional circle or wider society, we become far less attuned to the idea of changing things for us. We lose our focus on what matters, we get caught up in a way of being even if it is misaligned with our true values and intentions.

Is it time for you to reset and refocus? Is it time to breathe and smile knowing you have got this? Are you ready to create a sense of peace, purpose, and positivity? Our time is finite on this earth, let us use it well.

2. How to Use this Book

'When we actually choose the direction
of our thoughts instead of first letting
them run along the grooves of
conditioned thinking, we become the
masters of our own lives.' Eknath
Easwaran

I will encourage you throughout to prepare for
the changes that will make a real difference to

you. To get the best out of this book, it will help if you are:

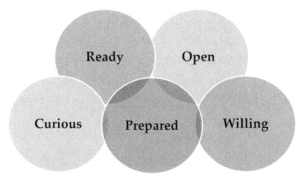

- READY to reflect
- OPEN to exploring your personal situation
- CURIOUS to generate new insights
- PREPARED to create new perspectives
- WILLING to consider making changes

By refocusing you can overturn the feelings of hopelessness and helplessness. Whilst you might feel blocked or overwhelmed right now you can tackle the big stuff by breaking it down and deciding what to pay attention to rather than getting immersed in thoughts that are unhelpful and unkind to yourself. By tapping into your innermost thinking and generating new unique insight, you can be your best self, more of the time, and start living your best life.

As the unpalatable saying goes, 'How do you eat an elephant? One chunk at a time of course!' Five Ways to Focus© is structured to help you chunk up your thinking into bitesize pieces for your busy brain. In each chapter you can expect:

- One **big question**
- **Five ways to focus** on that question
- **Insight questions** to prompt some deep reflection and create clarity.
- **Action questions** in each chapter will help you make plans for a positive way forward.

Getting the Best from This Book

You can make this book work for you; all it will take is a commitment to work with the questions and take a look inside yourself. By opening yourself up to the process, you will find this is a transformational experience.

You may choose to read through the book in one go initially and then return to answer the questions one section at a time. Alternatively, you may want to engage with the exercises and complete the questions in each chapter as they come up. There is a handy worksheet on the resources section of my website for you to record your answers

https://www.ontheupconsulting.com/finding-ways-to-focus/ Or a notebook will be useful.

It might be helpful to revisit the Five Ways to Focus on future occasions whenever you notice that you need a greater focus on the things that will make the biggest difference.

Checking in with the approach again, is a great way to coach your own life when overwhelm resurfaces or new situations present themselves. Of course, your answers and actions may change over time.

Slowing Down and Noticing

 When we have a head full of bees and can't see the wood for the trees, when our mind is a muddle, we just need to pause, take a new look, and get a fresh perspective.

Try This:

Here is a first step to practicing focus that will help you tune in to yourself. You can find this as a guided visualization on https://www.ontheupconsulting.com/finding-ways-to-focus/

When we are overwhelmed, it can feel like we have a head full of bees. Buzzy thoughts like a swarm of busy bees that flit around zigging and zagging in the hive of our minds. The humming and zumming of unwanted thoughts can distract us from our inner peace. And unhelpful and disruptive thoughts can be like bees that sting us prompting a sense of unease or emotional pain.

Here is an exercise for practicing focus, a bit of mindful brain gym that will help you tune in to yourself. Find yourself a quiet place away from distractions. Get comfortable, and take a few deep breaths, relax and picture this.

Imagine yourself as the beekeeper, you oversee the bees. The hive is a place of energy, noise and activity. You imagine yourself slowly turning down the volume, as if you were tuning out from the noise of busy thoughts. As the sound fades to a distant hum, you choose instead to listen only to your breath. Cool air comes into your nostrils and warm air leaves your mouth.

As you listen to the air coming in through your nose imagine the space in your mind getting larger. With your mind's eye explore the space and enjoy the peaceful feeling of openness. Your chest rises with the in breath filling you with nourishing oxygen, then falls with the release of the exhale. You let go of thoughts and distractions and focus only on the sensation of the breath.

As thoughts come to mind notice them but do not let them linger, let them pass like clouds. You don't need to keep track of them. They do not need your attention right now, thoughts will come, and thoughts will go, everything comes to pass.

Now, picture yourself as the beekeeper, at a safe distance, you are well protected. You know how these bees, these thoughts behave, but you are well prepared and will not be stung.

Imagine now that you are surveying the scene. You start to focus. You see the blur of yellow energy, notice the gentle hum. Trace the path of one of the bees.

See, that bee settling on a fragrant flower. Gaze upon its golden fleece as it brushes against delicate pollen.

Watch mesmerized as it moves with purpose and attention on to the next bloom. You are, enticed by the vibrant colour, attracted by the scent.

Observe the bee repeat this process. Notice how the bee plots its path according to the rewards along the way.

See how the bee is purposeful, directional, measured. Have regard for how it is undistracted by the wider world, but intent on gathering nectar for its honey.

Reflect on how your thoughts are becoming intentional and focused. Your thoughts that are worthy of your attention can set you on your path and can bring the outcomes that you seek.

Only quality thoughts deserve a place in your mind. Notice how much easier things feel when there are fewer things to focus on and when you pay attention to the things that matter most.

Over to You:

Now that you have slowed your busy mind, from this new space, we can encounter the Five Ways to Focus with a sense of readiness. Take some time to read the sentences below, and then when you are ready insert your own words in the paragraph below.

1) The reason I want to focus more is because I often feel...

2) I am looking for...

3) to help me be more...

4) and have more...

5) this is important to me because...

Excellent! In completing this exercise, you have

1. Stated your current position

2. Noted what you want to be different

3. Set out your intention.

4. Brought into sharp focus what you want and

5. Been clear about why these matter to you.

You now have the building blocks for the rest of the book. These are your first five ways to focus. Let's discover more.

3. Finding Focus When You Need It Most

Do you find yourself talking while texting, googling while zooming? Have you been known to juggle the TV remote, phone, and tablet with the dexterity of a roller-skating octopus serving soup while whitewashing a wall! Multi-tasking seems like a clever way to be productive. However, it is a modern-day myth! We cannot be wholly engaged in more than one thing at a time and so we end up giving only selective attention to most things instead.

Our focus on the things that really matter is becoming more infrequent and our interactions with real people are of poorer quality. We forget to look for depth, meaning and valuable experiences. Our focus is scant and superficial.

Our cognitive processing when multitasking actually reduces productivity by up to 40%. It can lead to mental blocks and fatigue from switching between digital distractions. This false sense of performance is an illusion that belies the token interactions and tick box outputs we are all engaged in. But knowing what things do not really deserve our time and energy and learning to focus on a few important things, rather than too many insignificant things, is a way of being that takes discipline. We can retrain our brains.

In this chapter, we will explore the Five Ways to Focus as a mental model that will help you to cultivate your attention with absolute intention. Retuning our thinking to focus on what we need to see and understand more clearly helps us understand the changes we need to make.

The Big Question

What is taking up too much of your attention?

To answer that fully you will need to zone in on the things that are stealing your sense of mental ease. We can use these five ways to do that by focusing on understanding:

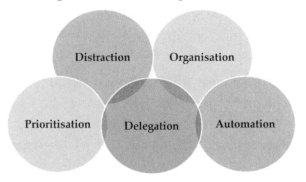

1. **Distraction**
2. **Organisation**
3. **Prioritisation**
4. **Delegation**
5. **Automation**

Way to focus 1: Dealing with distraction
Just Checking

Seventy-one percent of us never turn our phones off. Typically, people check their phones on average every 12 minutes during their waking hours with almost half of us doing so within five minutes of waking. Our phones are our lives - or so we think. It is a paradox that we believe our phones give us peace of mind by providing us with connection to others, useful information, timesaving and convenience, when in fact we have cultivated an over-reliance on these devices. This means we feel we cannot be apart from them and are devoting huge amounts of our precious time to using our devices.

Many of us value constant connection as convenient communication and have traded it for the time and headspace we actually need to relax, recharge, and review our thoughts. We are thinking fast more often than thinking slow, so we are operating most often without emotional depth, without regard for what we really need and want. We have become more operational and transactional and less relational.

The constant ping of notifications and rapid update of statuses is making us hypervigilant leading to digital fatigue. This is an emotional state that is both unsustainable and unhealthy and akin to anxiety. The 'always on', 'always accessible' and 'always responding' culture means we are only a click from our work emails before we go to bed, one scroll away from a work report on a Sunday morning or just a single swipe away from seeing someone's 'insta-perfect' life when we are our lowest moments, creating a cruel contrast to our own chaos and confusion.

FIVE WAYS TO FOCUS

'Where Attention goes Energy flows; where Intention goes Energy flows!'
James Redfield

Being bombarded by information from the start to the end of the day makes it difficult to know what to pay attention to amidst the distractions. Juggling work, home and family demands and commitments, trying to keep up with friends and social engagements, and being accessible 24 hours a day takes its toll. We find ourselves spinning around on a mad merry-go-round of life, with the music playing at super-fast speed. We are unable to catch the words, nor listen to the tune or see what is really going on around us, we are just trying to hold on and not fall off. If our attention is drawn to a million things a day, are they the things that matter most? Are these things draining your precious energy that you want to reserve for the fun stuff in life? The stuff that lights you up that is you, you at your best?

Consider your commitments

We can only truly get clarity by slowing down and paying attention to what matters otherwise it is a bit like trying to count cars as you drive at 70mph on the motorway. There are most likely some things that regularly get in the way in a very full but not necessarily fulfilled-feeling life. We all have genuine demands from our responsibilities, commitments, and of course dependents.

Whoever you care for, or are responsible for, whoever depends on you; whether that is your partner, children, older relatives, and pets (or all of the aforementioned), undoubtedly and deservedly, these create significant draws on our time and attention.

It is good to check in and use a Goldilocks technique to see if you are doing too much or just enough and who else can help. Try asking yourself whether you have the balance 'just right' or if you need to adjust, pull back, engage some more support, or find a different way to 'help'. Understanding how involved you *are* in these demand areas and how much you *need* to be involved will highlight if time and energy are being well spent, if you are the best person to help and whether you must keep doing it all, all by yourself.

Just as you would check your bank account for any direct debits for services you pay for but no longer need, the same applies to us in life. We might be tied to commitments which are no longer in our area of interest or responsibility. Remember that these are optional. You decide. Perhaps if you are feeling over committed, now it is time to decide if these commitments are a distraction from other things you want to or *have* to do. You could do a quick check-in with yourself and ask if you have served your time well and is it time to move on and create space for someone else to step up. One example might be if you find yourself still on the Parent Teacher Association of a school your children left 10 years ago or are still arranging the Christmas Carol Concert in a village you moved 60 miles away from 12 months ago. Saying no can mean someone else will say yes.

Whilst we might have to accept in our lives that we have responsibilities, and dependents, we have the freedom to *choose* our other commitments.

Drama - a Source of Distraction

Something else that causes us additional distraction is drama. I don't mean the latest soap opera or the National Theatre's popular performances; I mean the drama we create and court.

Drama doesn't just
appear, you either make,
attract or seek it. Ask
yourself is this a role you
really want to play.

You might be surprised to see how much of your time and energy is taken up with events that are no more serious than storms in teacups but attract the same level of attention as a hurricane in a Hornsea Pottery factory.

 Check in and notice if
you are fretting and
sweating about things
you are not actually
responsible for.

If you find yourself joining in with other people's sideshows, ask yourself whether you really need to get involved and play a part or can you stand by.

Be clear about what else you already have to deal with. If you can handle the distraction that other people's drama brings then great, but when you are already over-burdened, then think about how you can best 'help'. Is there a way to support without adding your own emotion to the situation? Can you support without shouldering the load, bringing it home and adding it on to the stuff you already need to sift through yourself?

My husband has a great expression- 'tend your own garden!' If it does not concern you then why are you getting involved? There is wisdom in this, and in knowing how to practise a self-disciplined way to clear your headspace by keeping a focus on what you are responsible for and not losing sight of this.

You can still listen and be a good friend while minding how involved you need to be and investing emotionally only what you can commit to. Do you really need to take on or sort someone else's stuff when you have not yet done anything about your own?

When you cultivate a better focus on your own things that do need your attention you will be in a much better position to help and listen and be there for people you care about. So maybe you owe it to yourself and those you care about to focus on tending your own garden first.

Build Boundaries to Deal with Distraction

Perhaps the previous section left you thinking 'well that is easier said than done'. Here you will see how to make that happen. It is all about building your own boundaries and sticking to them. Boundaries are a good thing to have, especially if you are a farmer and want to keep your sheep safe from wandering amidst the cars and motor homes careering up the A1.

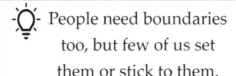 People need boundaries too, but few of us set them or stick to them.

Even fewer of us let others know what our boundaries are which makes it even harder to apply them in practice. When we are kind enough to ourselves to set our limitations about what we will and will not and can and cannot commit to we can be clear about our limitations. We can be honest about what we are available for, and to who and when, instead of being overcommitted and emotionally worn out.

This way we really own our space in the world and show up in a way that keeps us psychologically safe and allows us to engage positively with others on our terms.

If we set reasonable expectations of ourselves based around the time that we have and the energy and skills we have, then we are much better at focusing that time on the people and things that matter to us most and not frittering it away responding to everything that comes within our line of sight.

I get it. Really, I do. We like to people please, and it feels good; we like to be liked and to think we are good old souls. We even get a little hit from our feel-good hormone dopamine. Our little angel's wings start to bud and our halos have a little buzz and glow about them. It feels nice, oh so nice, to be helpful and kind. It feels good to be wanted and needed. When we have the mental space and time and energy it feels right too. But when we are already overtaxed, over-burdened and overwhelmed then the effect does not last long, and we return to an unhappy state sometimes even feeling resentful that we didn't pay attention to our needs first.

In-flight safety briefings remind us to put our own oxygen masks on before helping anyone else with theirs. Making sure you are in a good and fit state yourself is the best way to help others. This means learning how to say *'yes'* less and thinking about you first.

Setting boundaries and being clear about them with others is important. We can check first with ourselves what we are about to take on and whether there is another way to help or to help the person help themselves. Even if that means saying 'no' sometimes or 'not now' you will still be special, always, I promise! You will have made a conscious choice of what to focus on.

Insight Questions- Distraction

1. What are your biggest distractions?

2. What would life be like if you were able to manage these distractions?

3. What are the commitments you no longer want to be involved with?

4. What boundaries do you need to define and apply for yourself?

Way to focus 2: Organisation
Create Organisation

I promised this book was not going to be about becoming uber-productive but let us at least try to work a little wonder on the mental clutter in our busy brain. To do this I will need you to be honest. Yes, it is confession time, though just between you and I, no judgment, no penitential prayers, no need to seek forgiveness from a higher power, I promise. Do you regularly lose things? Ok, so if the answer is yes then, you are most definitely losing focus. No doubt about it. All those occasions when you lost your keys, purse, phone, password, or could not lay your hands on important documents add up to a loss of focus. Not just the time spent looking for those elusive items but also the negative mental narrative that runs through your mind whilst you are frantically searching. Let us explore a typical scenario.

It is 7.50 and you are ready to leave for work the train is at 8.05 and it takes 10 minutes to walk to the station.

The keys are not on the sideboard and could be in any number of different places. You search different coats, pockets, and bags. You rush upstairs, admonishing yourself as you nearly trip over a stray pair of shoes. You ask your partner accusingly whether they have seen the keys and dash back downstairs before they have time to answer.

You discover the keys while rummaging through the laundry basket. You notice it is overflowing, another job you've not got round to yet.

You check your watch. It is 8.01! No time to walk to the station so you decide to travel by car. You feel stressed that you will be stuck in traffic and likely to be late again. On top of all that, you feel guilty about the unnecessary pollution of that short journey.

As you pull away from the house, reaching for your phone to set it to bluetooth you realise it is on the dressing table. You feel shameful and flustered. You are not in the best frame of mind for a meeting with the boss about your pay rise.

The more you can organize the things that matter and that you need regularly the better you will be able to focus on what is important. You will save time and energy and be more positive about yourself and your situations. Creating habits about where you put essential things you use every day and routines will help.

Preparing in advance for important events will be a great way to be more organized, forward-focused, and feel better about yourself. Having apps that save your password and having important documents scanned in and saved securely can save you time and stop those dreaded feelings of bewilderment and frustration.

Insight Questions- Organisation

1. What do you need to organise to have better focus?

2. How could you do that?

3. What would change for you?

Way to focus 3: Prioritisation

We forget sometimes how much choice we have about what we do and when. If we find ourselves just dealing with whatever comes up as it arises then chances are we are working towards someone else's priorities rather than our own.

 Whenever you can, prioritise what matters to you first. You will feel better about what you are doing and where you are headed.

Making a list of what is on your mind and then determining what needs your best and most urgent attention and what can wait is liberating and sharpens your focus as you see the order of action needed. It also stops you from carrying it all in your brain taking up much needed headspace.

Beware of Busy

What value do you place on the word busy? For some of us being busy is connected to our view of our self-worth. It is not a particularly healthy outlook, but our society prizes busyness. Of course, laziness is not a desirable trait but there is a whole continuum between busyness and laziness, and we should not assume a binary view, it is not a matter of one or the other. Nor is it helpful to assume people will think badly of us.

Busy is good if you are feeling productive, purposeful, and that you have enough to keep the cognitive cogs turning. However, when the level of busy tips into overload and stress it might be time to check in and see if being busy is a reaction to a fear of being seen as or perceived by yourself as lazy or not valued or not important. Understanding your connection to the word busy and whether it is something that helps you and is something you want to sustain, or if you want to make a shift to a better, more balanced way of being.

> ☀ When you notice what you are so busy with you can decide how important it really is.

Remember that your work is not related to your personal importance even if society tells us it is. You can choose how you feel about yourself regardless of the perceived importance of your work. Your self-worth starts with how you value yourself first not with your role. Even donkeys have a day off (as my mum always says). Perhaps you want to click the busy button to 'off' and give yourself a chance to reset and refocus.

Determining what is right for you and what you can do with your available time and energy makes a difference. It is about noticing when you need to relax, reflect, and reset in order to be more focused and emotionally balanced.

Procrastination

Procrastination is the antithesis of prioritisation. When you look at the things you have been meaning to do and have not yet done, try to assess how important those things really are and what is stopping you. There may be a deeper reason why you have been putting things off. Assessing whether you have what you need to get things done or identifying what is holding you back will help.

> Perhaps there is something you need to overcome first before you can tackle the task that has been taunting you with its incompleteness.

For many of us it is fear of failing or fear of what other people might think, or even fear of being too successful! Many of us hesitate about taking the next step towards what we want as we are often more concerned with what we perceive others might think of us. We imagine the worst kind of criticism. We place our happiness in other people's hands, and this limits us and stops us initiating the first action even though *we* really care about achieving the ultimate outcome.

Starting by naming and labelling what you think is in your way is a good way of being able to understand if there are any beliefs that are holding you back. You can ask yourself if those beliefs are true or not. Here is a way to name your shame about the *not doing* and get a wriggle on!

Remind yourself why this is still important to you *or* for you, have a positive word with yourself about not holding back from the things that matter to you. Imagine the best things that will come from this and ask yourself who will be in your corner and support you. Then you can move from the thinking to the doing.

Insight Questions- Prioritisation

1. What are you too busy with?

2. What are you too busy for?

3. What do you need to stop procrastinating about?

4.   What has been stopping you?

Way to focus 4: Delegation

Applying a new focus of prioritisation also means that you might see what you can delegate. You might be able to identify someone else who could take on the task by asking yourself, 'if not you then who?'

Delegate with Diligence

Often people are reluctant to delegate for different reasons. It is time for some myth-busting now! Here are some of those reasons why people are deterred from delegating and how to counteract them so you can delegate with diligence:

Reason 1 - Being Precious

'No one else can do it as well as me.'

Counter-argument

Everyone is as good as their brief. Make it your job to find the best person for the task, understand their strengths and establish if they have the capacity for an extra piece of work. Explain what you expect, by when. Outline what will help them do a great job and if you will be available should they have any questions. Ask what they else they might need from you and agree what you will do to support.

Reason 2 - Being Overly Responsible

'It is my responsibility; I should see it through.'

Counter-argument

It is ok to ask for help when you need to. Perhaps you cannot do it all alone. That is why you are overwhelmed and reading this book; you want to find ways to do less and have more focus on what is important, so does something have to give?

 No longer assuming responsibility for things in their entirety without considering the parts others can play will shift your inward focus on the problem to an outward-facing look for a solution.

Learning to share responsibility for some things with others may help you. Few big projects are completed in isolation from others.

Acknowledging the help you needed and received is also a way to train your brain to see when you might need help again and where to find it. Plus, you will be able to make a better case in the future about what is needed for success on a piece of work to ensure the outcomes are of high-quality and achieved on time and you perform at your best.

Reason 3 - Assuming

'Everyone else is too busy!'

Counter-argument

You do not want to add to someone else's load and perhaps you assume everyone else is busy without even checking if that is true. When you do find a person who has the time available to support you to get something done, it can be surprising to see the opportunities you might generate for someone else to learn and grow or feel valued. You might find a way to champion and reward this person and help them step up along their career path and vouch for them with colleagues now you know what they are capable of. So, this way you do get to be a superhero as well, albeit indirectly!

Insight Questions- Delegation

1. What are you holding on to?

2. What can you delegate?

3. Who can you delegate to?

4. What difference will that make to you?

Way to focus 5: Automation

Carrying everything that you need to remember in your brain is both exhausting and unreliable. It can also make you emotionally unavailable as your left brain is highly activated with the critical processing information you need to get through the day and the language and emotion centre in your right brain is less alert.

Is it time for you to embrace technology to automate repetitive tasks? Using apps for contacts and diary management is the simplest way you can manage your focus. If it needs doing it needs to have a person or time allocated to it.

So rather than just, jotting something on the to-do list, or popping it on the ever-growing pile of post-it notes, or lodging it in that overstuffed mind of yours, how about dedicating it the time and resources it deserves?

One effective way is to put everything, and I mean *everything* that you need to do in your e-calendar. As soon as you know that something new or additional needs doing, create a diary entry.

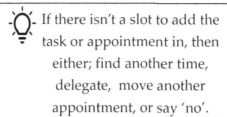

If there isn't a slot to add the task or appointment in, then either; find another time, delegate, move another appointment, or say 'no'.

It is as simple as that. This approach can give back a sense of control and make sense of what you can manage and what you need to focus on daily and over time.

When you think about what you need to do frequently and repeatedly it will be helpful for you to find an app that can systemize that for you. Anything that pings you a reminder, for example, an exercise app telling you that you have a run scheduled tomorrow, will mean that you don't have to constantly remind yourself.

Insight Questions- Automation

1. What can you systemise to help you focus?

2. Do you have what you need to do that?

From 'Too Much to Do' to Knowing What to Focus on

You have moved through the fog of too much to do towards knowing what needs your attention. This will serve you well and help you to feel lighter, freer, and more focused. Maybe you are now closer to being able to answer the big question. *What is taking up too much of your attention?* These action questions will help you reflect on this section and enable a deeper understanding of what it will take to work through some of the knots that have created confusion and you can organize the overwhelm into a clearer, calmer way of being.

These changes may take a period of adjustment and you may not find them easy to apply at first but reminding yourself why they matter will help and applying the actions you create below will take you forward.

Action Questions

1. What do you need to change most of all?

2. What will you do less?

3. What will you do better?

4. What will you do more often?

5. What is the first thing you could do that would make the biggest difference?

4. What's Going Well?

You are a whole person who is affected by the goings-on in all aspects of life. You have decisions and choices to make and are constantly balancing the demands in different domains. We can feel weighed down by this and it can block us from finding ways to enjoy what we have or to change things and move forward towards what we want. We keep trudging on, keeping going but missing the adventure that is life; things feel jaded. Sometimes it can seem more about getting through each day rather than enjoying a life of joy and purpose.

When did you last look at how your life is as a whole? Sometimes we get caught up in thinking about how hard everything is and tell ourselves things like,

'Everything has gone wrong!' 'My life is a mess!'

Whoa! Hold up there now! Did you know that our brains believe what we tell ourselves the most? It is called mental conditioning.

When we put all our energy and our thinking time into focusing on the problems, we overlook the things that are going well and forget to think about what we can do. We lose sight of the smallest possible changes, the first steps that could take us forward. We come to believe our internal rhetoric of how truly terrible everything is. Our emotive language about the situation and harsh thoughts condition us to believe it is true, and we like to think we are right. Those limiting beliefs then go unchecked and unchallenged, and we get stuck.

The more we think negatively about our situation the more we affirm a sense of our difficulties; we feel literally weighed down and highly sensitive to anything else that may add to our troubles.

Let's look afresh. Has *everything* gone wrong? Really? Is your *whole* life a mess?

> It is by noticing the good stuff and appreciating it that we also create the courage and curiosity to peer into the elements that might be creating difficulties and generating overwhelm.

We will focus on five aspects of life, keeping you at the centre, noticing if certain aspects are going better than others, in order to answer the big question.

The Big Question

What is going well and what could be better?

The chances are there will be some questions here that will highlight areas that you have not noticed are truly wonderful! (How great will that be?) or pretty good (that's going to help too,) as well as noticing the areas that could be better and are worthy of your new attention and focus.

The five aspects of life to focus on are:

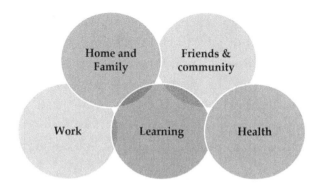

1. **Home and family**
2. **Friends and community**
3. **Learning and development**
4. **Work**
5. **Health and wellbeing**

Way to focus 1: Home and Family

When your home is just the way we want it to be, the family are all doing great, and relationships are healthy and happy at home we feel good about ourselves too. However, home and family stuff can be tough and can affect us in lots of ways.

We are spending more of our time than ever in our homes for study and work. Your home may be a place of sanctuary or a place of chaos but noticing how your home feels to you is important. By taking some time to think about your home you can become clearer on how well it works for you and what might need to change. If you have enough space and enjoy the space you have then that will help. But if you struggle to relax because your attention is drawn to the things that need fixing or changing then that will affect your ability to access inner peace when inside your home.

'Home is where the heart is.' Gaius
Plinius Secundus

Relationships between loved ones can be tricky and at times wonderful. Relationships evolve over time and families grow and change. This can bring new demands on the people who live together and sometimes a shift in the dynamics can leave you in a spin. Perhaps you haven't thought about how much space each of you need and how you can be happy in each other's company too. This is where you check-in and consider how things are working for your family and relationships at home, giving you a chance to get some clarity and determine what's going well and what could be better.

Insight Questions -Home and Family

1. How would you score your home and family life out of 10?

2. How does your home look and feel to you?

3. How are the relationships at home?

4. What are the family or relationship changes you are experiencing now or need to prepare for?

5. What do you want to change or improve about your home?

Way to focus 2: Friends and community

Our social interactions can make a difference to how we feel about ourselves and can be either a source of overwhelm or support depending on the quality, mutuality, depth, and frequency of these connections. Many of us are spending time transacting with people online, comparing ourselves with others allowing ourselves to be influenced by other people, and feeling judged or inadequate. We are spending less time strengthening the bonds with the people we really like, love, and trust, and focusing more on people who matter less to us than our real friends.

Maybe you have some great people in your circle who you enjoy spending time with and with whom you share life experiences. We are naturally social creatures so being with people who you can be your true self with might be important to you. Having people who make you smile, and who you have strong bonds with that survive difficult times matters to many of us.

You might be active in groups that have a really positive influence on both the people they serve and each other. Perhaps you have hobbies, interests and are involved in community activities. Or maybe this is an area of your life that you have been neglecting and have withdrawn from for whatever reason. Think about the people you spend your social time with and the community you are connected with and involved in.

 Notice if the balance feels right and if you have enough time and focus on this area or if it is neglected as other aspects of your life have taken precedent.

Let's explore now how well these things are going.

Insight Questions -Friends and Community

1. How would you rate your life with your friends and community out of 10?

2. Who do you have a strong sense of connection with?

3. Who brings out the best in you?

4. What do you feel you need more of or less of in your friendships?

5. How much time do you have for your interests?

Way to focus 3: Learning

'If I want to improve my situation, I can work on the one thing over which I have control - myself.' Steven Covey

You may be studying to be a neuroscientist or learning to crochet. You might be on a professional development programme working towards a qualification or accreditation, or preparing for a promotion. Alternatively, you might be advancing through personal development, like mindfulness practice, or by being coached. Your learning may come from growing avocados on your kitchen windowsill in Altoona or starting a sensational sourdough in downtown San Francisco.

> If you thought learning was something you only did at school, then perhaps this deserves some attention now.

Every day brings a new opportunity to learn; remember we are all works in progress; you have the chance to be even more amazing if you seek opportunities to advance. You might notice you are in a bit of a rut as regards your development and sensing that you are not developing skills and knowledge or experiencing new things.

So many of us get stuck and forget to look at what we can do to grow and develop. We lose our forward focus and stagnate like a murky mill pond, flowing nowhere, bound by the reeds of inaction.

If this, is you, let's see where you could put your focus to find ways to show up and shine in the world, (or even in your spare room where you will get great at playing the guitar or establish an exciting new business! Whatever works for you!) It is time to gather your insights to sharpen your focus.

Insight Questions - Learning

1. How would you score your learning out of 10?

2. What would you like to be able to do?

3. What would you like to be better at?

4. What would you like to learn more about?

5. What would this learning help you to do/ achieve/ become?

Way to focus 4: Work

For most people work is their major source of income. However, earnings are not the only way to measure whether work is working well or not for you.

 We need to look closer to find out what work means to you. Work at its best can bring happiness, success, connections, friendships, security, and fulfilment, and fund the lifestyle you desire.

You might be in a good position where you are suitably rewarded and challenged in a positive way. Or at the other end of the spectrum, you might feel that work is an aspect of life where you are unhappy, undervalued, deskilled, or overly challenged and under-resourced.

Considering that we spend around eighty thousand hours in a lifetime at work, it makes sense that we want to enjoy it. For many people, their experience of work is tough, and it is getting worse over time. The Chartered Institute of Personnel and Development studied 6000 workers in 2020 (pre-pandemic) and noted that for some people, work was having an increasingly negative effect on their well-being and work-life balance. Notably, respondents cited: regular exhaustion, unreasonable workload, excessive pressure, and described how the pressure of work made it hard for them to switch off and relax in their own time and not being able to fully enjoy their home and social lives.

 It is futile to fear failure in things that don't matter to us.

We stay in roles for lots of reasons even when they are not working well for us. Often, we fear that:

- We will lose the security that we perceive the role gives us. (So we soldier on and try to be thankful for what we have but resentment can build and resurface).

- We will not find another job. (So we don't try looking).

- We will be letting people down. (We deny ourselves our happiness and become less engaged in our work and make less effort.)

- We should be happy with what we have even if we know we are not. (We keep going until someone else decides on our future with a restructure or redundancy or our working days come to a natural end).

The pandemic proved that many of us can work from anywhere. Employers are downscaling their large corporate property base and encouraging flexible, hybrid working arrangements. The traditional employment model is changing; freelance workers are set to make up 50 per cent of the workforce in the US by 2027. The portfolio career - in stark contrast to the 'job for life' that previous generations prized so highly, is on the rise. People are discovering ways of making work and life balance beautifully, blending things they love to do with things that pay the bills.

Even before the pandemic people were starting to re-evaluate their lives, to revise their priorities, sensing that they now have the permission to plan new ways of how to work and live their best life. The remote working mandate in response to COVID-19 has meant we now know work will probably never be the same again (yay!).

You might be sensing the itch you need to scratch. Perhaps you are at a change point, courageously contemplating a career change but have not had the chance to work out what it would take and make the bold steps. Or you might feel the heat of the boiling point at work and are ready to lower the pressure and rediscover work joy. Here we will check-in and see if your work works well for you and see what needs to change.

Insight Questions - Work

1. Why does work matter to you?

2. What score out of 10 is your work right now?

3. Why?

4. What is the thing about your work life that you most want to improve?

5. What would be the impact if you could improve your work life?

Way to focus 5: Health and Wellbeing

It is easy to take our wellbeing for granted and believe that these amazing machines – our bodies and our supercomputer brains, will go on forever without us needing to be assured that they have what they need to function at their best. A significant proportion (between 20% and 40%) of illnesses suffered in the Western World are preventable and are primarily caused by lifestyles. We have a choice to make - to take notice, or to carry on and hope for the best.

People are living longer, it is true, but people are living with more life-restricting conditions than ever before.

We believe we can
have it all and do it all,
expecting our minds
and bodies will deal
with all we throw at
them.

In truth though, we need the right balance to live long, happy, healthy lives. We need a greater focus on what helps keep us healthy. If we managed our work lives better, we would end up with fewer stress-related illnesses. Are we taking for granted that the health services are there to fix us if we don't take care of ourselves in the first place?

'Every human being is the author of his own health or disease.' Buddhist proverb

The evidence tells us that if we ate more whole, fresh foods, fewer saturated fats and red meat, we would suffer less from digestive disorders and diabetes. If we took regular exercise and fresh air and had good sleep we would age better, function better, and restore our body's natural balance.

> ☀ We would be our own
> health creators,
> preventing the misery
> that illness brings and
> generating wellness
> and vibrancy.

I guess you knew that already. The thing is we do know what to do. We know we need to take care of our health and well-being, nevertheless while we are busy being busy it can easily slip down the list. Here you can focus on your health and wellbeing and see what insights you come up with.

Insight Questions – Health and Wellbeing

1. How would you rate your physical well-being out of 10?

2. How would you describe your level of emotional wellbeing?

3. What do you need to pay attention to as regards your health?

4. What would that change?

5. Why would that matter to you?

From Inner Wisdom to Applied Action

So, what did you notice about your own home and family, your learning, your social and community life, work, and your health and wellbeing, - what would you say is going well and what could be better?

Your insight here should help you to answer the bigger question of what is going well and what could be better. Not all bad? Some things going well? Great!

 Take a moment to feel content about the good stuff you have generated, created, cultivated, and been gifted within your life. With that inner peace a new space will open up enabling you to apply a finer focus on the things that could be improved.

With this wisdom, I believe that you now know what to do. Providing your answers to the action questions will clarify in your mind what needs to happen next. In later chapters you will use what you have brilliantly called into focus here to: make practical plans for what is possible, keep the good stuff going, and to work on what needs to be better.

Action Questions

1. Which aspects of life are going well, and which need your attention to improve?

2. What is the first thing you will do?

3. What will it take to make that happen?

4. What difference will it make to you?

If you would like to explore these aspects in more depth you can access a life audit tool at

https://www.ontheupconsulting.com/finding-ways-to-focus/

5. How to Get Things on the Up

'Successful people maintain a positive focus in life no matter what is going on around them.' Jack Canfield.

Our thoughts fuel our feelings, and our emotions drive our behaviour often without us even noticing what triggered that reaction. Refocusing and tuning into our inner wisdom is actively choosing what to bring into our consciousness. When we regularly focus on things that make us feel good, it stimulates the neural signals to remember that we liked it and it made us feel positive emotions. These signals act as sub-conscious reminders to seek out more good things to create that reward effect time and time again. It is all about activating the Reticular Activating System (RAS) in the brain.

Think of the RAS as an inbuilt search history that generates advertisements for things that your brain knows will get your attention. Effectively, the more time and attention you actively give to something, you condition yourself to think about it more often, the more this part of the brain computes that this is what matters to you and will attract your attention to that subject or situation in the future.

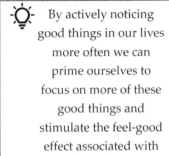

By actively noticing good things in our lives more often we can prime ourselves to focus on more of these good things and stimulate the feel-good effect associated with them.

To be positive in our outlook we need to dig deep and actively look for the good in our lives and inside ourselves to help us feel mentally strong and hopeful about our own future.

> *'Look well into thyself; there is a source*
> *of strength which will always spring up*
> *if thou wilt always look.' Marcus*
> *Aurelius, Meditations.*

Conversely, if you spend your time focusing on what makes you unhappy or the most negative aspects of your life you will condition your RAS to keep advertising these things to you, like a film reel that has the highlights filtered out and instead features the worst bits of the film as this is what your innate processing system thinks you want to see. The brain is like a computer, working on the basis that input + process = outputs. If you fill your mind with negative thoughts and focus on only the difficulties your brain will process this to show you more negatives than positives.

The Big Question

How do you feel about how things are going for you right now?

I appreciate that might not be easy to answer at first, I mean where do you start? Five Ways to Focus as a framework can bring forth your insight and clarity.

In this chapter we will discover what you are:

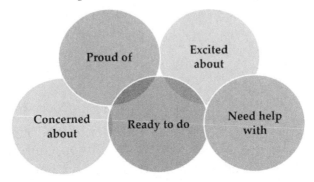

1. **Proud of**
2. **Excited about**
3. **Concerned about**
4. **Ready to do**
5. **Need help with**

Way to focus 1: Proud Of

What are you proud of? Noticing the things that matter to you and how you played a part in bringing them into your life is a good thing and yet is often overlooked. If it makes you smile or makes your heart swell, then bring it to mind and admire it. Focusing in this way regularly may help you find ways to bring more things into your life to be proud of.

When we are aware of things that are going well, we tend to feel better about ourselves and our situation. Too often though we forget to give ourselves a little pat on the back for what we have accomplished. Personal pride is often associated with being conceited and the phrase 'pride comes before a fall' is quoted to deter anyone from getting too big for their boots. No-one likes a boastful braggart, but I am guessing that if you are already aware of this then you are not likely to become one.

 It is about showing gratitude to yourself by recognising your own personal impact and ability.

You don't have to get yourself a t-shirt printed that says 'world's best mum' or present yourself with employee of the week every Friday. (Although if you run your own business and are the sole employee, heck, why not, maybe that will help and who needs to know?) You go and do whatever it takes to keep yourself motivated, don't be afraid to shine, and be a champion for yourself.

Whether you are pleased with yourself because you logged off from work in time to make a delicious healthy meal, buoyed up by that morning run you managed to make time for, or proud of the way your child dealt with a really tricky situation at school, it all adds up. So now it is time to note down all the reasons to be pleased with yourself and make that pride list. What are you proud of?

Insight Questions- Proud Of

1. What fills you with pride?

2. What happens when you notice the things you are proud of?

3. What does that tell you about yourself?

4. Is there anyone you would like to share your pride list with?

Way to focus 2: Excited About

Having things to look forward to in life makes a difference in that they can drive us forward. New experiences build new neural pathways, increase our problem-solving abilities, improve our mental agility, and keep us positive and hopeful. They help us learn how to take risks and shift from the perceived safety of the comfort zone towards opportunities for change and personal growth.

During the COVID-19 pandemic people were locked down and restricted from doing and planning the things that would normally keep them going. Not having things to look forward to and plan like holidays, meals out, cinema trips, theatre outings, music performances, or sporting events meant that people felt flat. Every day was like Groundhog Day for months, with people feeling they were not thriving, just surviving. We need hope in the form of excitement. With a sense of excitement, we feel more alive; adrenaline keeps our brain firing, our hearts full and our cells ignited.

Without hope, we can stagnate, give into boredom, and stop seeking the fun things in life, the stuff that gives us positive energy for creating meaningful experiences.

Insight Questions -Excited About

1. When did you last feel excited about something?

2. What are you excited about in your future?

3. What else could you be excited about that you have not given much attention to?

Way to focus 3: Concerned About

How often do you ask yourself, how you are doing?

'I'm fine, I'm OK, I'm just busy. I'm just tired.'

So often this is our response when someone asks how we are. Perhaps we do not pay enough attention to how we are feeling from moment to moment, from day to day, from week to week.

We just keep going and then it builds up and we notice that we are not really fine at all. Not just busy, not just tired, but actually completely overwhelmed and struggling to keep pace with all that which demands our attention.

When we reach this point *everything* gets more difficult, we teeter on the edge of the burnout zone. We are less able to deal with the tough stuff, our resilience is lowered, our capacity to cope is challenged, our relationships suffer, our productivity and quality take a tumble.

 'Warning! Crash ahead' flashes like a motorway sign but often we do not pay attention and just keep going anyway.

It may be small things that concern you and niggle away and perhaps need some quality attention to deal with them. Often these thoughts pop up when you have a moment to yourself, or when you lie your weary head on the pillow at night. 'Pow' in they come, those little pesky thoughts that create a restlessness and disturb our inner peace.

Your concerns might manifest as a sense of unease about a situation you are in, you notice it at the time and perhaps even react to it with irritation, or maybe you push it away because you don't really want to face it. Maybe these things that concern you keep flaring up. The hot buttons are pressed and before you know it you have lost your temper.

I encourage you to think about how you are. To dig a little bit deeper, to understand yourself a little bit better, and to give some focus to what concerns you. This will help you move forwards with a true perception of the obstacles that obscure your focus and thwart your progress.

'It is essential for you to remember that the attention you give to your action should be in due proportion to its worth.' Marcus Aurelius.

Having the time to properly understand what is going on for us is important. Making time to consider our concerns and face our fears makes a difference. It puts you back in a state of emotional control and rational thought, you create the inner peace to move lightly through your life.

Knowing what needs our attention and noticing the things that we can genuinely pass off as unimportant is about having the emotional intelligence to know your triggers and how to react in a way that is better for you, your relationships, and your health. It is a skill.

The way to hone that ability is to notice in the first place when things bother you and then make an active and conscious decision on whether this is something that requires some rational thinking applied to it or if you can rely on the emotions that show up at that moment to help you navigate a way forward. How can you be sure you are making the right decision when you are feeling emotional?

When we know how we feel about things, this can help us decide whether we need to do something proactive and positive to move towards greater success and personal happiness.

Doing nothing can even be an active choice. Not reacting in the heat of the moment but refocusing and choosing responses that line up with your values and how you want to be, will help.

Insight Questions- Concerned About

1. What are you concerned about?

2. Why is this a concern to you?

3. Would it be helpful to you to give this thing more attention or less?

4. Are you reacting to this concern in a way that is good for you?

5. Do you have what you need to deal with this?

Way to focus 4: Ready to do

Throughout this book you have been answering questions- lots of them, and perhaps the answers that you have come up with are already sparking seeds of an idea that you might need to cultivate further to live more of your best life and be your best self more of the time. A farmer always clears the land before he plants new seeds to give those crops the best chance of success.

When you clear your mind, you know what to focus on, you are free of distractions and concerns and can be prepared for the new. So, what are you noticing now that you might be ready to do? You may be starting to think about making a small change or getting ready for a fresh start. Perhaps you have been putting off something important, but with your new insight you now feel ready to take the first step, maybe the time feels right, and you are more prepared now than before. Living in lockdown created life-changing experiences that certainly jolted people's consciousness and caused many of us to reassess our lives.

Perhaps you have had your own life event that has sharpened your perception. Those boiling points and change points can really be the times to take notice and make a shift. Recognizing that you are ready to make the changes for a happier, more fulfilling, and more balanced, and successful life is a great start.

Lessons from Lockdown

We can choose our own lessons from the lockdown in response to the COVID-19 pandemic and decide what we do with that new knowledge, but not everyone will have used this lockdown lens to focus and provide an indication of what they are ready for. Some of us just want things to go back to normal, but in doing so we might miss what could be better and different, and what changes we could make for ourselves. Returning to normal actually means moving backwards.

Your future is partly about taking lessons from the past, knowing what you are feeling now and how you want to be going forwards. We need to accept that some things are changed forever; we can never go back in time. By focusing on what we know now and using that wisdom to plot a way forward we can be clearer on what changes we are ready to make.

Insight Questions-Ready to Do

1. What is that thing you have been thinking of that could take you forwards?

2. What has changed to make you ready for this now?

3. If you do act on this what will happen?

4. Why does that matter?

5. If you do not act on this what will happen?

Way to focus 5: Need Help With

The next step is to notice what you may need help with. Asking for help is not something that everyone is comfortable with, and you may see it as a sign of weakness. It takes courage to ask for help. It is also a demonstration of your commitment to improving yourself, an act of self-love, an indication that you value yourself and want to be your best self. Sometimes you are doing all you can, but help is needed.

Now, what is wrong with that? It is something many of us struggle with. Sure, it may be cringe-worthy to say:

'I'm not feeling great at the moment.' Or:

'There is some stuff that is really bothering me right now.' Or:

'I don't know how to do this.' Or:

'I can't do all this on my own anymore.'

Imagine for a moment how the other person may feel delighted that you asked them. You might make their day. You may even help them help others too, once they realise that people find their help useful.

Too often not asking for help leads to more overwhelm so having some ways that we can reach out can make the idea seem less daunting.

 Noticing when you are at your limit and there is no longer enough time, energy, or solutions available to you is a good signifier that you need someone else to get involved.

Being ok with asking is one thing but being prepared for, *"No, sorry I can't help with that."* is important too.

The first attempt at reaching out may not get you what you need or may only be a temporary solution. Finding the right person and the right help may take several attempts. Some help may be better than no help until you find what works best for you.

Focusing on what you want help with, and for how long, and above all being clear what that help should enable you to do will alleviate some of the difficulties you face.

Insight Questions- Need Help With

1. What are the things that are keeping you stuck?
2. What do you need help with specifically?
3. Who could help you with that?
4. What would happen if you no longer needed help with this?

From Self Knowledge to Practical Action

Hopefully, your Five Ways to Focus has clarified how you feel about how things are going for you. You now hold a deeper insight about: what you can be truly proud of, what excites you about the future, what concerns you, what you are ready to do, and know what help you will need to get things on the up.

Action Questions

1. What is your first step towards these actions?
2. What will be the most positive thing about being aware of these five ways going forwards?

6. What Are You Really Looking For?

Perhaps you have never taken the time before to think about what you are looking for. It may be the case that your situation in life has changed recently or is about to. People often come to me for coaching when they need to decide about a life change that may be a career move, promotion, retirement, or setting up in business. Or when life has already thrown them a curveball and they are wanting to reorient themselves and discover how to get things on the up again.

Life's transitions can be
disorienting and
knowing how to make
good endings of the
things that are no longer
available to us is
important, and can help
us consider new
opportunities with eyes
wide open to make good
new beginnings.

People can feel overwhelmed by the choices in front of them and want to know where to put their focus in order to make plans for a positive future. During these transitional periods, I help clients to understand what they truly seek and what drives them, helping them to focus on what lights them up inside.

The Big Question

What are you really looking for?

To pursue something that matters more to someone else than it does to you is to deny your own happiness and success. Caring for people, raising families, and supporting children to thrive and prosper can be hugely rewarding and may be the happiest times of your life. Pursuing the goals of the company and supporting the ambitions of your boss or shared goals of a team can also bring satisfaction, career advancement, and feel fulfilling too.

But what if you are missing something? What if there is something else you now seek. What if you can no longer ignore that *niggle in your noggin* of knowing that? A waking knowledge may have recently dawned on you that says, 'Hey what about me? Is this my time to shine?' It may be precipitated by a life change; children starting nursery or school, or growing up and needing you less, a demanding relationship ending or a new one that creates space for you beginning. Or when the boss moves on, or the company gets taken over, and suddenly you realise you have shelved your aspirations for too long and now it is time for a rethink and a refocus.

> *'Man is pushed by drives but pulled by values.' Viktor Frankl*

You may realise you want to focus more on yourself and what matters to you but don't know where to begin. If you are experiencing one of these situations or similar right now, then this will be a great chapter for you to see what you want in this next phase of your life.

When I use these Five Ways to Focus with coaching clients to help them see what they are really looking for, I encourage them to assess where they have been focusing and invite them to place, Fellowship, Kudos, Money, Freedom, and Fulfilment in their own order of priority.

We sometimes forget that we can choose, and we have more control than we realise. Deciding for ourselves what to focus on, is one of the best things we can do for ourselves and the people that depend on us. With these five ways in mind, we can explore the answer to the big question and discover what you are seeking.

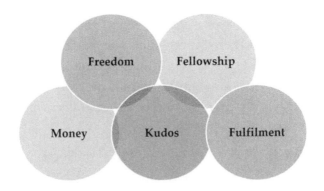

1. **Freedom**
2. **Fellowship**
3. **Money**
4. **Kudos**
5. **Fulfilment**

Try This Task

Place each one of the five words in order of what you think you value most. Try not to overthink it; allow your first impression to come to the fore, unchecked, no need to overthink it. In the remainder of this chapter, I will explain each one in turn and you may want to check back and revise your list according to what each one then means to you with your renewed focus. As you read on, try to think about what is driving you to look for a change in your life and what you seek more of.

Way to focus 1: Freedom

Perhaps you want to break away from something that feels wrong or difficult right now, or you may want to experiment and try something new using your strengths and your skills.

In your current situation do you have enough freedom? Perhaps you are in a job where you are free to manage your diary enjoying flexible working hours, flitting seamlessly between work and home, feeling the freedom of a truly satisfying work-life balance. Maybe you like how you can choose who to work with. You might be working freelance and enjoying the satisfaction of choosing the clients you want to work with and working in a way that truly suits you, where you don't feel micro-managed or overly scrutinised. Or maybe not, and this is now prompting you to think about the commitments and restraints you currently have and what you might be missing.

If you have recently retired or taken a career break you might notice that it is not more freedom that you seek but less. Freedom might have brought you too much choice and downtime and you are seeking a more structured way of spending your time. Maybe you want to consider whether you are ready to trade free time for more responsibilities or commitments.

Insight Questions - Freedom

1. What does freedom mean to you?

2. Do you want more or less freedom?

3. What would that mean specifically for you?

4. How would that change things for you?

Way to focus 2: Fellowship

What about fellowship? For many of us having a sense of belonging really matters and is right up there in the Maslow Hierarchy of Human Needs as it can provide us with the psychological safety we need to not just survive but be at our best. You may get your sense of fellowship by being part of a community of like-minded people, or in a team where you feel valued and connected, or a group of friends with whom you share interests and wonderful experiences, or family with whom you share close bonds, positive experiences, meaningful connections, and cherished memories.

Being part of something that feels special, feeling connected to a cause that stirs you, can also mean that you have a sense of fellowship. You might be a member of a mutually supportive community of like-minded people. Napoleon Hill described how one of the secrets of success amongst some of the greatest industrialists of their time in the 1930's was a Soroptimist group, now often referred to as a mastermind group.

This concept has stood the test of time and is used to level up success by sharing ideas and offering support in a group of carefully selected trusted individuals who each have their expertise and experience and who commit to helping each other to progress and fulfil their potential. A group where individuals are valued, for their knowledge, contributions, intellect, compassion, or shared experience. Considering whether you are well connected to the people that could help you generate more of what you really want can bring about some interesting insights.

Can you talk about the things that matter to you with your friends and family or do you find yourself closing down and not sharing your ideas, achievements, and frustrations because you think they won't get it or won't want to know? You can live in a house-full of people and feel lonely if you are not connected emotionally with each other by talking about the things that matter to you.

Now that fellowship is in the landscape of your conscious thinking, is it an area that could do with more focus? Do you want to be amongst a network or team of people, that care about the same things you do, who can support you, and who you too can offer something to? Or do you have this covered and know that you have enough contacts, collaborations, and companions already?

Insight Questions - Fellowship

1. How important is fellowship to you?

2. Where do you get your sense of fellowship from?

3. Do you have positive connections with people who care about the things you care about?

4. Who would be in your mastermind group?

5. Are you well connected to the people that could help you generate more of what you really want?

Way to focus 3: Money

Money is still a taboo topic in 'polite' conversations in many cultures and is synonymous with secrecy, control, and power. This has led to significant financial illiteracy even in our modern world.

With financial planning having been the natural domain of men for generations, this has held women back from understanding their worth and gaining the financial rewards they deserve from the work they do. Shamefully, significant inequalities still exist between women's and men's pay.

 No one can afford to be ignorant about their financial position in terms of their current lifestyle or their aspirations.

Women's financial insecurity can be a factor for staying in abusive relationships. Being, unable to support themselves and their children financially on their own can trap women in miserable, unsafe situations.

Having a positive relationship with money includes being aware of how much income you need to either support your current or future situation. There is a correlation between money and happiness. For many it can make life easier but too much money can bring too many pressures and decisions that have the converse effect. Again, the Goldilocks principle applies. What will be just right for you?

Is this a time in your life when you feel that with the right amount of focus you could generate the income that will make the difference to you and your family? You might sense that there are things that do matter to you but are currently unaffordable and more funds would enable you to afford the things that until now have been beyond reach. You may be making money but spending too much and not saving enough, changing this would make a difference to your future.

Some of the simplest, most pleasurable things are free but perhaps you find you have been chasing down the high earning roles and not getting chance to enjoy the simple pleasures, the real rewards.

Life changes bring about new demands on our finances. For anyone who finds themselves with teenagers, the prospect of supporting them through university can be a daunting prospect and not everyone is prepared. Being blessed with a new baby may fill you with joy but the prospect of paying for full-time childcare or taking a pay cut on maternity leave may fuel fears about finances you have not had to face before. Providing financial support for elderly care may also be a concern. Life's changes bring new financial considerations.

Maybe you have experienced the loss of a job and without savings, you are struggling to make ends meet. Money seems like a slippery subject, but is best not avoided, and should be kept under regular review as life changes occur. What you have and need now will be different from what you have and need in the future. These questions will help you take stock and see whether you are comfortable with your money situation or if it warrants some greater insight and action by bringing it into focus.

Insight Questions - Money

1. How would you describe your relationship with money?

2. How financially secure are you?

3. Do you earn enough for the work you do?

4. Do you earn enough for your lifestyle and current expenses?

5. Are you preparing for future financial requirements?

Way to focus 4: Kudos

Maybe you are looking for kudos. Is it about time you were known for something? A time where you stand in your truth and are recognized for who you are and what you do. Does this whole idea give you a buzz or repel you? Kudos is about being recognised for something you do. These might be the things you are best at, the things you can do more easily or better than most.

Understanding what this means to you at this point in your life and whether you are driven towards it, is worth focusing on. For some, the very idea of kudos or recognition is a daunting prospect and is so far down the list of desirable elements in one's life that it is certainly not sought after and perhaps avoided at all costs. For others, they are happy to be in the spotlight and it meets their needs to promote their offer, become known, appreciated, accepted, and needed.

Social media has given people the opportunity for recognition beyond being a legend in their living room to having access to the planet in a pocket. People can easily join community spaces and share their views and content with a global audience of billions. When you take time to think about what you want to be known for, and who can benefit from what you know or can do or have done, you can determine whether it is something you want to or need to pursue more actively.

You can be clear on whether it will bring the rewards you seek. Imagine if Louis Pasteur or Thomas Edison had not shared their inventions and discoveries with the world for fear of being known and applauded for it. While you have been busy perhaps you haven't noticed the value of the things you have done or created. Would it be useful to share those things with a wider community? I wonder what would happen if you did, perhaps your knowledge could change the world even in a small way.

Insight Questions - Kudos

1. How important is it to you to be known for something?

2. What do you want to be known for or stand for?

3. Who could benefit from you sharing what you know or can do?

4. How does your online presence align with the way you want to be seen professionally and personally?

Way to focus 5: Fulfilment

Now, what about fulfilment? Being fulfilled in life is when you know you are on your path, your life has meaning, you can see the difference you make. You regularly feel contentment and satisfaction and you feel rewarded by the results you create.

I can spot when someone is fulfilled, they carry themselves differently. They have a little spring in their step, a smile on their lips, a song in their heart... (No? Really?) Well, try it for yourself. Who do you know who seems to be fulfilled? Look at their demeanour, there will be an ease about them, a sense of satisfaction, not smugness, not bravado or conceit, but a quiet knowing that they are congruent with their true selves.

They will be leaning in to embrace life with their whole heart and using their beautiful brains. They know instinctively where they are going and what they do, like metal knows to follow a magnet. Their heart and their head are working well together as a perfectly integrated system. They enjoy what they do, they put their best selves forward, and get the results they value. Not only does this matter to them, but they also get their meaning from knowing they make a difference to the people or causes they care about.

There are said to be three types of people in this world, those that make it a worse place, those that make no difference, and those that make the world a better place- no matter how great or small their contribution is. Which kind of person are you being right now? Perhaps you are lacking fulfilment and you are not getting what you need so you are finding it hard to give. Perhaps you are or have been in a situation or role where you have lacked purpose and it has not felt rewarding to you.

> When we feel unrewarded, or undervalued we are less likely to show up and give things our best.

And if the world is full of people who lack fulfilment, then it stands that there is a whole lot less contribution to the greater good being made. In coaching I often work with clients who have found themselves at a change point or boiling point. In these situations, it can be the case that the client realises they are no longer driven by what mattered in the past but are now driven towards the greater fulfilment that comes from knowing they are on *their* path and living *their* life's purpose, fulfilling expectations of themselves because they matter to them, and not feeling undue pressure of other people's expectations.

Here the rewards (accomplishments or status) they have been seeking up until now, may seem less valuable and unimportant. They realise the emptiness they feel is because they were never their own goals, they were someone else's goals set for them. They were not intrinsically motivated to achieve them but extrinsically influenced towards something that didn't actually matter that much to them themselves.

Clients sometimes feel at a loss when they come to me. It is not uncommon for people to be floundering, unsure, not knowing where to turn because every path looks either too arduous or pointless. Unfulfilled people may question who they really are and how they can serve their purpose. When we lose our connection to our purpose, we question what the point of our existence is.

Yet when these clients look to their unique talents and strengths and explore the opportunities for work or activity that creates true meaning for them, they know what they feel driven to be and do. They feel and value the benefits and end up giving more by showing up with purpose and making an active whole-hearted contribution. Bringing what matters into focus is truly transformational for many people.

Are you noticing now whether you want to strengthen your focus on fulfilment and seek more opportunities for greater meaning in life? Or do you now know that this is something you already have and are very grateful for?

Insight Questions - Fulfilment

1. What gives you a sense of fulfilment?

2. Do you seek greater fulfilment?

3. Do you know what to do to feel more fulfilled?

4. How would that change things for you?

5. Do you know how you could achieve that?

Driving Forwards with Focus

What have you been driven by up until now? Perhaps you have been chasing financial rewards, but now the money is not enough, and you want fulfilment from a more meaningful role. You know that the job has taken its toll and you now know you want to spend more time with family or friends, so focusing on freedom with a more flexible work role is going to be a greater priority. Or maybe it is your time to step out of the shadows and showcase your strengths and be known for what you can do and care about. If so, then kudos is going to be higher up on your list.

You might like to return to the list you created for the task at the start of this chapter and list the five ways in the order of your new priorities now knowing what you want to focus on going forwards. You may have noticed that one of these aspects is in short supply right now and a future life of abundance would mean more freedom, kudos, money, fellowship, or fulfilment. You decide how to work and live in the ways that make you happiest. In the following chapters, you can see what is possible and start to make your plans.

From Insight to Action

To know what you are drawn towards is true self-knowledge, to commit to pursuing it is not purely self-serving or self-indulgent as it will help you to show up in the world and do your best work and make your best contribution with your individual authentic self. The action questions which follow will get you on your path towards what you truly seek.

Action Questions

1. Now that you know what you seek more of, what is your first step?

2. Knowing that some things are not that important to you, what will you do differently going forwards?

7. What is Really Possible?

Being Positive on Purpose

Being purposefully positive means focusing on the things that we *can* do in our lives, and the things that we *can* change. If we spend our time thinking about how difficult everything is; how stuck we are, how we are all out of options, how unhappy we feel with our situation, and what we cannot control or influence then this limits us. A shift in perspective helps to take a view of what is possible, especially if you want to discover your true resourcefulness for getting things on the up!

Here we build on your insider knowledge of your very own self to focus on the things that need your active attention. These Five Ways To Focus on possibilities help my clients to understand what they already have in place and what requires their attention to make more good stuff happen. Helping people see the strengths they have already can also stretch and challenge clients to keep reaching higher to achieve what they know in their heart and their heads will make a difference to them.

Earlier we looked at what was going well and what could be better. Often, we ignore the signs that tell us we can do something to change our situation.

 Sometimes we feel a little tense about the idea of moving forwards and taking the steps that will bring about real change because even a place of stuckness becomes comfortably familiar over time.

When we become resigned to our problems and dismissive of possibilities, we risk accepting what is not good enough, and resentment grows.

> *'We cannot control what happens to us but we can certainly control how we react to it.' Maya Angelou*

Occasionally, we think others are responsible for our problems and we regard the view through this blame-tinted lens as the full picture. We fail to see what else *we* can do to change how we regard a situation or to respond differently. In these circumstances, we do not recognise where we have the scope to act to change things.

Being Curious

I encourage you, to notice the good stuff and what can be even better. You can bring possibilities forward into the mind's eye and challenge yourself to view a situation afresh. To step beyond the problem towards possibilities is to free yourself from personal judgment, layer up with self-compassion, and be ready to see what this will bring.

The Big Question

What is really possible?

The Five Ways to Focus

To answer this question, we will focus on five ways to identify what you can do to get things on the up.

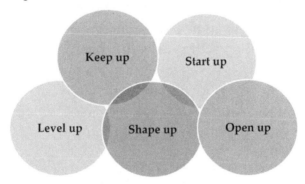

1. **Keep Up**
2. **Shape Up**
3. **Start Up**
4. **Level Up**
5. **Open Up**

Way to focus 1: Keep Up!

What is working well right now and how can you do more of it? Refresh your memory of what is going well in those important aspects of your life and try to recall what you did to create that little bit of fabulousness happen. By taking stock of the good stuff you do and making a commitment to keep doing it *you can* feel more purposefully positive and attract even more abundance.

Have you been great at getting up earlier this week, tip-toeing down to the kitchen to fix yourself a green smoothie, and secretly write the first 10 pages of your debut novel, while the rest of the household sleeps, savouring that tranquil time all to yourself, rather than oversleeping and scrambling to find clean clothes and lunchbox items in a whirl of mayhem and madness to get the children to school and yourself to work? Well, done! Now, how can you keep it up?

Or maybe you have been working on your social media presence, posting relevant and compelling articles about your work, and attracting just the right kind of clients and keeping your business in flow. You can value that too. Note it all down, all the good stuff, and remind yourself of the things that are working well and helping you to be winning at life, acknowledging even the little things.

Notice them here and set your intention that you want to keep these things up because they are working and can create firm foundations for your positive positioning toward becoming your best self. Writing down what is going well, attaching value, and commitment to it will help you stay motivated, and you will be positively powered by your current success to keep up the good stuff. I am excited for you!

Insight Questions – Keep Up

1. What is working well right now and how can you do more of it?

2. How will that change things for you?

Way to focus 2: Shape Up!

What is going ok but could do with some of your attention to make it so much better? Here we will focus on the things that may have escaped your attention, but you do want to improve because they matter.

> ☼ If things are not going well in one aspect of your life, they do have a habit of affecting other parts of your life if left unchecked or unchanged.

For example, when there are problems at home, they can affect how we feel about our work and vice versa.

Problems can be both energy-draining and time-consuming, so allow yourself to focus here on what you identified could be better in each aspect. Also, if you know you have slipped out of some good habits recently like eating well, exercising, and getting a good night's sleep then these could be great areas to turn your attention to and decide what you can do.

Shaping up is an antidote to that sneaking sense of shame when we know we could do better, but don't do anything about it. So how about it? What will you focus on to shape up? What do you want to get better at in your day-to-day? Or looking further ahead, what do you want to shape up to achieve your bigger, wider plan for living your best life?

Insight Questions – Shape Up

1. What is going ok but could be awesome?

2. What differences could you make by shaping things up?

Way to focus 3: Start Up!

I get it, until now, you have just not had the time to focus properly and fully consider what it is you want to start doing for yourself because you have been giving your time and attention to all that needs to be done to keep the show on the road at home, or keeping those plates spinning at work. Or your focus has been on pleasing everyone else or just getting through each day.

 You deserve better and
your best self knows this.
To make a change we
need to make a start, and
to make a start we need to
make a change!

This means changing how you think and being hopeful by focusing on possibilities and your true potential. This is about committing to thinking about what you want and what you are prepared to do to move things forwards for you.

It might be a small step, for example committing to a new exercise routine that takes you towards a healthier lifestyle, or a big step, for example starting up a business and going freelance or putting yourself forward for that promotion that you have talked yourself out of before.

 If there is something you can't go a day without thinking about perhaps that deserves some real attention and a new level of focus.

There are probably some brave new things that you've thought about, but you haven't committed to doing. Too often we dismiss things before we fully explore what it will take to make the good stuff happen. Dreams are dismissed before they can take form, ambitions get archived in the 'one day, maybe' folder in our busy brains or worse the 'forget about it' file. Hopes are thrown around like hoopla rings at a fair, with you unsure where they will land or if you'll win your prize.

People at the end of their days often say they wished they had lived their lives a little more fully, taken more risks and worried less about what people might say or think about them. So, what will you start up? What are your own hopes, dreams, ambitions and what can you start to do to work towards them with boldness, and courage? Your future self will thank you for your focus and commitment.

Insight Questions – Start Up

1. What are the brave new things you could start to do that would make a real difference to you?

2. What will it take to get started?

Way to focus 4: Level Up!

There are some things, I guess, that are going ok for you, but you may have reached a point where you can go no further without increasing your knowledge or skills. Perhaps you are at a point in your career where your promotion prospects would improve if you were able to demonstrate competency in a certain area or had a particular qualification. I prompt you here to think about what you want to level up. Essentially what can you do to achieve that? Once you know what you need to learn, discover, and understand you can put your focus into finding the ways to doing that. You will grow!

So, this is where you make that list of things you want to learn and get better at to achieve what matters to you. It may be something you can learn from a colleague or friend or from an online tutorial or it may be a more formal route to learning through professional qualifications. Either way, here you can notice it, name it, and commit to your way of levelling up to reach your own goals. You got this!

It might be important for you to focus on what you can level up if you have not been using some of your skills for a while and you believe that you have become less able. People returning to work after maternity, paternity or carers' leave often worry about this. The important thing is to notice it, test out if it is true or just a fear, then find ways to rebuild confidence.

A lack of familiarity with something that used to be so commonplace can unsettle us so if you are feeling rusty, trust me - taking action to restore your confidence is a strategy that works far more than ruminating on what is not working which will further wear down your self-belief. So, what are you looking to level up, discover and learn more about to get things on the up for you?

Insight Questions –Level Up

1. What do you need to learn more about to take things to the next level?

2. What results would you like to create?

3. Why does that matter?

Way to focus 5: Open Up!

Sometimes we keep things bottled up too much. We don't share our concerns, our hopes, or our aspirations. This can make us feel blocked. Understandably there are times when we don't want to discuss how we feel and often this is because we don't trust how that will be received or we don't feel ready to be honest about our feelings. Sometimes we just do not have the words.

So, we put things off, we don't face them, we pretend they are not really there or not important to us and we repeat the thinking patterns that limit our potential and allow concerns to fester, forming the knots that tie us to a way of being that is a smaller, constrained version of ourselves.

Being open and honest with yourself firstly about what you want and then sharing that with a trusted group of friends or family can lead to you asserting your ambitions. It can help you bring forward the possibilities available to you. Once these people know what you care about and are seeking to achieve, they will most likely support and encourage you in your aspirations. If not, then perhaps they aren't the right people to talk to.

You may have some real concerns, currently, and these might be on a scale spanning niggles and worries to something that is keeping you up at night. Society is starting to acknowledge that good things can come from being aware of your emotional wellbeing and people are starting to accept that talking about what troubles you is not a sign of weakness but can foster good mental health habits.

> *'Talking about your feelings isn't a sign*
> *of weakness. It's part of taking charge*
> *of your wellbeing and doing what you*

can to stay healthy.' - Mental Health
Foundation

If you have got in the habit of sidestepping the things that bother you and side-lining the things you care about, then opening up could start with journaling to get your thoughts in order. You can see what feelings you attach to those thoughts and how that leads you to behave in certain situations. You may see a pattern in your thoughts and emotions.

A bigger step might be to find someone who will listen without judgment, someone who cares enough to understand why this matters to you and will give you the space to explore what concerns you and help you see your options and possibilities.

Sometimes the things that loom large in our minds are less threatening when they are given a good airing. We can feel unburdened. A client once told me that what she liked best about our sessions was that she could get her thoughts out of her head, discuss them, make sense of them and then figure out what she needed to do. So how will you open up about the things that matter to you and who will you turn to?

Insight Questions – Open Up

1. What do you need to be more open about?

2. What do you hope would change as a result?

3. Who could you trust to share your thoughts, feelings, and aspirations with?

Using these simple concepts as your prompts to bring into focus your possibilities and potential, will help you grow, shine, and keep moving forwards in ways that will make the biggest difference to you. Next, we will turn to specifying actions and timescales so you can really commit to feeling more fabulous, being more brilliant, and achieving your ambitions.

Action Questions

1. What will you do to keep up the good stuff?

2. What will you do to make a start on something new?

3. What will you shape up and improve?

4. What will you level up and learn more about?

5. What will you be more open about?

6. What difference will this make?

8. Action Stations

You have done a lot of the important work, by filtering through the mental clutter and now we can turn our attention to the small steps that will move you forwards. This means homing in on the specifics now. Nope, no more dodging the issue by lingering in the lagoon of contemplation, no matter how tranquil that feels, it is action stations time. We will step things up a gear here and masterfully put into play practical actions that address the big question.

The Big Question

What will you do to get things on the up?

Rumination Gets You Down

Ruminating about things that we could be doing (because every moment should be filled of course! Or so we think!) Or should be doing (because we think other people expect it of us, but it is not the stuff we care about!) can create so much internal negative energy, it is draining. It can even lead to us cultivating our very own sour sense of shame and fetid feeling of failure! Which is so not good for the soul!

The actions that we talk ourselves out of taking, but are so within our reach, are our missed opportunities and our untapped potential. When we refocus and snap into action, get out of our own heads, stop paying attention to the inner critic and discover our inner coach and just get on with it, it can feel amazing!

Doing what you can do because it matters, means no more procrastination, no more scrolling through social media distractedly admiring other people's lives, no more looking back forlornly over opportunities that have already faded into oblivion. It means looking at the present and knowing how you feel and sensing what you want to shift. It is about using that inner wisdom to ignite your spark and get future focused.

You Choose What to Commit To.

This chapter includes five timeframes to help you focus on specific actions. As skilfully as spiderman scales a skyscraper, we will span across the things you can do almost immediately and scope out a view of the things you really want to be working on and achieving in the next year. I know you want to avoid the overwhelm that comes with too many commitments, so self-discipline applies here; I encourage you to choose what to focus on and only commit to what you think you can do.

People tend to commit to things more fully when the things really matter to them. When I say *commit*, I mean head and heart, fully invested, emotionally engaged, not just going through the motions, ticking the box, or being 'seen to be doing'. When we can imagine the benefits to ourselves or the people or causes that we care about, we are far more likely to be intrinsically motivated; all in, fired up, and committed.

Of course, it depends where you put your attention. If you mostly spend your time thinking about how tough things are and what you cannot do it will be hard to summon the self-belief to plan positive actions for yourself.

 One of the kindest things you can do to yourself is to cultivate your self-belief. This starts with seeing what you are capable of and what you can do right now.

The more often you do this the more you will build the muscle and create the neural pathways in the brain that make this recognizable as a rewarding and positive experience. So, what do you have to lose?

'People become really quite remarkable when they start thinking that they can do things. When they believe in themselves they have the first secret of success.' Norman Vincent Peale

Coming up with your own actions and stating a pledge towards them is therefore vital for you getting the results you seek. If ever a client comes to me and says they just want me to tell them what to do, I explain that is not the role of a coach. I don't advise; coaches help people explore what they want and need, they help clients examine the options available and actions they can commit to and are ready to act on.

Are You an Avoider?

You know when Netflix has a little pop up that says, 'are you still watching?' well the next time it appears see which you are most likely to answer.

a) Yes, ma'am, I am still watching. This is my chill time, no need for shame, or regret, I am not an avoider, I got my life together and this entertainment fix is just what I need right now.

b) Yes, I am. I know I have already clocked up 6 hours of viewing today, but that is only because I cannot face the real stuff I have to deal with.

So, which was it, a or b?

Or perhaps you suffer from analysis paralysis, where you spend so much time thinking about what needs to be done, but never quite seem to put the time into making it happen. Try to notice what it is that you spend your time doing rather than focusing on making things great and use these five ways instead.

So, let us uncover the insight you need now to move you to action and set the pace for you to keep moving forwards. Bring to mind for a moment all that you want to improve and achieve. It is all about your possibilities and your potential, discovering what is within your power, what you are capable of doing and what you can commit to.

The Five Ways to Focus

These are the five timeframes to focus on.

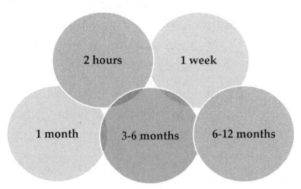

1. The next two hours

2. **The next week**
3. **The next month**
4. **The next three months**
5. **The next six to twelve months**

Way to focus 1: The next two hours

In the next two hours what could you do to help you get things on the up? There is no time like the present. And for us that like to procrastinate and avoid tackling what needs doing, this just might be the call to action you need. So, in the next 120 minutes is there anything you can do that will be good for you? Is there something that you don't usually do that you could start or try out? Is there something that you tell yourself you don't have time for that you could make time for?

Here are some examples of things you could do that might matter to you:

1. A ten-minute google search to see if your dream company is hiring.

2. A phone call to your boss to say that you are interested in a promotion and want to discuss the opportunities for moving up in the organization.

3. Looking up the application requirements for the qualification you dream about having.

4. A Facebook message to someone you have lost touch with who you want to reconnect with.

5. A short walk or dance around the house to your favourite tunes.

Whatever it is you get to choose and commit to a positive activity that means something to you. Now if you are reading this in bed just before you go to sleep, perhaps getting sleep is your priority, however what about on waking? Is there anything that you could do in the first two hours of the day that would change how you feel about things, something that you know would help you to be your best self?

Imagine if you began every day like this and became skilled at activating new opportunities by focusing on the next two hours as a timeframe of positive possibilities.

Insight questions – Two Hours

1. What could you do in the next two hours to get things on the up?

2. How will you feel if you do?

Way to focus 2: Seven Days

When you focus on the week stretched out ahead of you, what do you see?

For some they see more of the same, day in, day out, the daily grind Monday to Friday, and then a weekend tagged on to recover and get ready for the new week to roll around again. However, life does not have to be like that. Variety is the spice of life; such a cliché I know but if your routine has become humdrum then chances are you are stuck. Refocusing on what you do want to include in those seven days is a great way to start being intentional about making that happen.

Equally, if a look at the week ahead creates a feeling of overwhelm, then you have too much going on and it is time to think about what you want to focus on this week and what can be outsourced, cancelled, changed, postponed, or designated as not important.

I find that looking for the joy in the week ahead gives me a positive outlook. I either colour-code my diary for the things that I know will be joyful or I make a list of them and pin it on my wall. If I don't see enough joy in what I have planned, then I put more joy in. Yes, you can do this too. By adding in what makes you happy you make your week the kind of week you want to experience and stop being a passenger in your own life. You can start feeling like you are piloting the plane of possibilities to somewhere fabulous. You could inject more joy in the week ahead by planning to phone a friend, making something delicious for lunch, or reading something uplifting.

Insight questions – Seven Days

1. What could you do in the next week to get things on the up?

2. How would that take you nearer to achieving your goal?

Way to focus 3: The Next Month

A month may seem like a large chunk of time, but it is amazing how quickly time slips by when you are busy with other things. So, take the time to focus now on what you could do in the next 28 days to take you nearer to your goals, whether that is: your plan for a calmer, quieter life, a healthier lifestyle, a happier family, a more fulfilling way to spend your time, or your ambitions for a successful career. Perhaps there are things that you could do that you have been putting off for a while now, things that would make a difference if you put them into play.

In these next 28 days, perhaps there are some opportunities for you to start to get things on the up by taking action. How will you schedule those to make sure they happen? Little things count so include them in the list. Spread the tasks across the month and think about how you will keep track of them on a daily and weekly basis, ticking them off and creating new ones each month as needed, applying your focus to a rolling plan each month towards living your best life.

Planning a reward for yourself as you see the changes you are making can be highly motivating and is a key feature of sustaining behavioural change. So, you might want to consider how you could acknowledge and celebrate the changes you are making to positively reinforce your new way of being.

Insight questions – The Next Month

1. What could you do in the next four weeks to get things on the up?

2. What new habits and routines could you create?

3.   What might you need to overcome first?

4.   How can you do that?

Way to focus 4: The Next Three Months

Let's think a bit further ahead now to the next three months, a neatly sliced quarter of the year. If you were to imagine things being better in whichever aspect of your life, if you're looking to make a change, how would that look in three months? What actions would you need to take in that time to make sure that those important changes come about? Once you know the answers to this you will feel more propelled to put the things in place.

It might not be easy and there may be things that you have to face in the next few months. Considering the alternative can help you understand the benefits of making a shift and motivate you to act.

If you did nothing, would your situation get better on its own? This indeed might be the case, so your action could be to wait and see; you might need patience and fortitude to see things through and hope you come out ok on the other side. Or if you sense that you are underplaying your capacity to act and there are things you can do, then here is your chance to gather that insight and consider the actions to take you forward to where you want to be.

Accountability is important too for making a change. This may mean finding someone who you can share your plans with and asking them to check in with you regularly to see how you are doing. This could create the pull you need to keep going and create the life you want to lead.

Insight questions – Three Months

1. What can you do in the next three months that will be of benefit to you?

2. What would happen if you did nothing?

3. Are there any challenges you might face?

Way to focus 5: Six to Twelve Months

Thinking even further ahead, in the next six to twelve months, there are likely things you could do, but if they are not planned for, then they probably won't happen. Acting as if your success is in your hands takes courage and self-belief. Being future-focused is important to make the shift that will bring results. So, by looking to the longer term, you can determine how to activate those bigger plans. This is your chance to commit to some of the big things, the things that might be life changing.

If you imagine yourself being better at something in the next six to twelve months or having achieved something particular by then, then the time is now to make a start on planning how you will secure your success.

If you see yourself as a published author in twelve months, then now is the time to map out what it will take. Books don't write themselves overnight (believe me I know!) so spare yourself the disappointment of having another year pass and the goal not achieved and work out what it will take and what you are prepared to do.

Alternatively, you may know that your situation will change in a few months, perhaps with children starting school or going off to university. This could be your opportunity to focus on you with your new-found freedom. Planning for this now can help you make the most of those transitions and new beginnings.

If you know there is a restructure looming at work or a takeover and you do not see yourself as part of the new way of doing things then consider where you want to be and what you want to be doing. Some things in life seem like they just happen to us, but sometimes this is because we neglect to look further ahead to see what is coming at us. We forget to look within us to see what we want and what we are capable of.

Insight questions – Six to Twelve months

1. What can you do in the next six to twelve months that will create an outcome that matters to you?

2. Why does this matter to you?

3. Is there anything you might need to overcome first?

Your Time to Act

Is it really that easy to kick those avoidance tactics into touch and focus forwards? With practise it certainly will get easier, and the results and rewards will be yours to enjoy.

*'Your mind is your instrument, learn to
be its master not its slave.' Remez
Sasson*

Just as those *Choose Your Own Adventure* stories, popular in the 1980s, gave children a chance to select what happens next, you have this power now for yourself. Noticing what you can choose to do in these timeframes will supercharge you towards your next personal adventure however exciting and scary that may be. You decide.

Action questions

1. What *will* you do to get things on the up?

    a. In the next two hours

    b. In the next seven days

    c. In the next month

    d. In the next three months

    e. In the next six to twelve months

2. How will you make sure you act on this?

3. Who will you ask to help hold you accountable?

4. How will you know things are working out well for you?

5. How will you reward yourself?

9. Creating your Best Life

Freezing Fighting Fleeing

When we are feeling stuck, occasionally it is because we have got into some unhealthy ways of thinking about our situation and our perspective has become limited and our outlook bleak. We *freeze*.

Similarly, we sometimes feel the pressure so much that we move on quickly from one situation to another – a *flight* response. In our haste we forget to see what matters. We don't discuss things or try to work things out, we run. Often we make a decision too hurriedly and emotionally without rational thought.

When we feel threatened by our situation or the behaviours of others, we might react by fighting back. Losing our tempers and lashing out with words or actions, - the *fight* response.

These are psychological responses that naturally occur when we sense danger or difficulty. Responses that have been hard-wired into our brains over hundreds of thousands of years. Humans have always faced threats and these natural defence responses kick in automatically when we sense threats. These responses were really useful when we were cavemen and women where a sabre tooth tiger could be outside the cave dwelling at any point ready to pounce.

We have evolved and our social situations have changed and become more complex. We face different difficulties now every day. When these fight, flight and freeze reactions are in play our emotions run high and decision-making runs low. We often struggle to navigate the woolly web of work demands, relationships, commitments.

We feel threatened or undervalued and then make rash decisions to leave jobs, we feel insecure and unloved and end or sabotage relationships without thinking about the consequences, or we fester in miserable situations feeling powerless. There are always facts and feelings in any situation but at the key change points and boiling points it is common for people to discount facts, and act in ways that serve the present feelings more than the future desires.

We need to pay attention to how we feel about things that are happening to understand if we are responding in the best way possible. Most of us are not good decision makers when our feelings and moods are in the driving seat.

So how about we take a little pit stop, check in with yourself and see what you really need to think about to power yourself forwards. In either case when we shift our focus to the things that have made our lives rich and fulfilling, we can start to identify what we want to attract or create.

The Big Question

How can I create my best life?

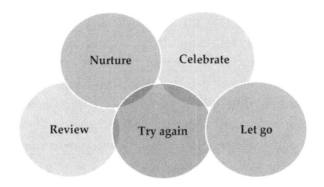

The Five Ways to Focus

1. **Nurture**
2. **Celebrate**
3. **Review**
4. **Try again**
5. **Let Go**

Way to focus 1: Nurture

When you think about the work you have done in previous chapters or as you come to this fresh, what do you know is so important to you that you need to keep it close? It may be a goal or ambition that you want to keep front and centre as you take your next steps. You may want to cultivate this and work on it until you are ready to share it and step forward to make it happen.

Maybe you want to invest some time into strengthening the bonds and creating a lasting connection with a particular person in your life. Perhaps there is a relationship that you want to nurture and help it to grow. You may realise that while you have been busy doing things, you have lost sight of someone that matters to you and now more than ever that person could do with a tender loving care approach that will benefit you both. Relationships are messy; perhaps there is something inside telling you to nurture something before it becomes beyond reach.

Insight questions – Nurture

1. What have you neglected recently?

2. What needs looking after because it matters?

3. What would happen if you were more nurturing?

Way to focus 2: Celebrate

During the global pandemic, lockdown restrictions prevented people from celebrating life events in their usual ways. No large gatherings, no affectionate hugs, no encouraging embraces. Congratulatory handshakes were shunned in favour of awkward elbow bumps. Good wishes were sent via virtual voice message and scant screen appearances. Birthdays were deferred and achievements were acknowledged in the most meagre ways. Award ceremonies appeared impersonal and hollow. New babies were born into a hostile world where we were all scared to hold, touch, and visit each other.

The lockdowns meant that we have been unable to celebrate in familiar ways that make us feel good. Celebrations have their roots in the most ancient of cultures and have continued to be important to people. Having a focus on the things you want to create in your life so that they can be celebrated in the future may be important to you. Noticing what is already there to be celebrated too is going to be helpful to you to build your wealth of happiness and sense of abundance.

 It is life-affirming to acknowledge the smallest things with a celebration.

Marking the moments and savouring the years are both impactful ways of drawing our attention back to what matters. Whether it is commemorating being five years sober or two years in business if it counts it is worth celebrating. Even celebrating the smallest of successes can be incredibly powerful as it brings a little high from the happy hormone dopamine and this trains the brain to want more of the good stuff. Noticing the good things cultivates a sense of gratitude and fires up emotional wellbeing with feel-good sensations. You can celebrate in small ways rewarding yourself for the little triumphs and overcoming the tribulations.

Simple ways to celebrate small things might include:

- **Keeping a bullet journal** of small good things and planning a reward for yourself every time you have 10 things listed to celebrate.

- **Ringing a bell**. Bizarre as it may seem, this has been a well-used technique in business, when a sale is made or a new client won, then the bell is rung. Chimes and bells can have a powerful affect in alerting us to pay attention to a positive occurrence.

- **Find an accountability buddy that you agree to share positive news with.** You may want to arrange between you to send an email every time something wonderful happens that matters to you or something particular in line with your goals. Together you can acknowledge and celebrate your achievements and happy events.

- **Take a look at the year ahead** and plan beyond the usual birthdays to mark your own milestones and think about how you will celebrate.

Insight questions – Celebrate

1. What deserves a celebration?

2. How could you celebrate small things in future?

3. What big things could you plan to celebrate?

4. What difference would it make?

Way to focus 3: Review

This book provides several opportunities to review how things are going in your life. At this point I invite you to get specific and choose one area of your life that really requires a good review. An honest appraisal of how things are and what is going well and what could be better. It is about taking time on your own to look inside and find answers.

The philosopher and psychologist William James, determined that attention:

> *'is the taking possession by the mind, in clear and vivid form, of one out of what may seem several simultaneously possible objects or trains of thought...It implies withdrawal from some things in order to deal effectively with others.'*

Being impartial about what we are doing, taking a helicopter-view, and assessing whether the way we are working, and living is the right thing for us right now is important. Consider whether this area of your life is giving you what you need and taking you where you need to be.

Insight questions – Review

1. What do you need to look further into?

2. What do you want to understand more about?

3. What might you find?

4. How might that change things?

Way to focus 4: Try Again

Not all is lost. As you have this opportunity to gather your thoughts, you may have ideas for things you want to try again. Perhaps there was something that you gave up on some time ago. Was there a dream you abandoned? Was there a friendship you neglected?

Was there a half-written manuscript or part-created invention or business idea that you want to revisit and reassess? We abandon things for so many reasons. And sometimes they are the right reasons and that is the right decision. Being true to yourself means being able to properly evaluate whether you gave up too soon, or whether you didn't put your heart into something, and it still matters to you.

If you can't stop
thinking about it
maybe it is time to do
something about it!

Think about why you gave up your idea or project at that time. Was it rejected for not being up to scratch? Did you discard it before it was good enough? Do you want to make it better now?

You may find that you are now in a better position to take forward that idea. You may have more knowledge now that may help you. Now may be the time to focus on that thing you never go a day without thinking about. How much do you care about this now?

Insight questions – Try Again

1. What are you prepared to try again with?

2. How do you know that it is the right thing for you now?

3. What outcome are you looking for?

4. What difference do you hope that will make?

Way to focus 5: Let Go

I take a lot of learning from the early stoics, the philosophers who believed that creativity, gratitude, joy, and hope were the cornerstones of resilience. The stoics firmly believed that all events are inert and neutral. It is we who determine events to be good or bad. The value and the emotions that we attribute to events can keep us stuck. We can find ourselves clinging on to things that are in the past that can no longer hurt us. We can multiply our misery by replaying and relaying situations where we have felt aggrieved or underappreciated. In doing so, we are capable of recreating the pain.

I heard a story of how a psychologist explained that if he asked a patient to recall a time when he had fallen and twisted his ankle then the patient could do that without experiencing the pain of the torn ligament and swelling around the joint. However, if he asked his patient to describe the time when he was humiliated by his bully of a boss then the patient would 'feel' the emotional pain again as if it were happening once more. He would feel hot, get sweaty palms and his breathing would become shallow and his heart rate sped up. That sounds to me like misery twice!

'Letting things go is an act of far greater
power than defending or hanging on.'
Eckhart Tolle

The psychologist warned that harm is done by and to us when we go over old problems and scrape at old wounds; instead, we need to work on what we are ready to leave behind in order to move forwards. Empowering ourselves to do this takes practice and does require creativity to see things from different perspectives, and hope or confidence that what happened before is unlikely to happen again. There is always a lesson tucked away in any difficult experience. We can be thankful that it did not break us entirely; feelings can be mended with new and happier experiences. This kind of gratitude is very empowering and helps prepare a more fertile ground for joy to sprout.

'Every person, if he is to have mental
health and live successfully, must move
away from past failures and mistakes
and go forward without letting them be
a weight upon him. The art of forgetting

is absolutely necessary.' Norman
Vincent Peale

So, it might be time for you to let good stuff grow and feel a lightness in your soul. This could create space in your busy mind and fewer emotional burdens. So, what are you now ready to let go of?

Insight questions – Let Go

1. What do you tend to revisit that is not helpful to you?

2. What are you considering letting go of?

3. How could you do that?

4. What would change for you if you did let it go?

We are never done; we are all works in progress. We have the chance to celebrate what we have and change what is needed. Reflecting in this way and focusing on the wonderful things, can help us gain a fresh perspective and make something precious. Trying again where something is worth saving, and letting things pass that cannot be changed or no longer serve you is a shift towards living your best life.

Action questions

1. What are you going to do to live your best life?

2. How will you overcome what might be difficult in making this change?

3. What is your first step towards living your best life?

10. It's All About You

You are a precious person who deserves to be their best. That might be nice to hear. Yet sometimes we behave towards ourselves in ways that run counter to what we need to be at our best and do things that are really not good for us.

Be Your Own Bodyguard

So many of us with our busy lives do not value our health until illness strikes and forces a stop. We may defer our own self-care and tell ourselves that we can look after ourselves later or that the doctors will help if we get really sick.

We ignore the signs and instead we keep going, keep doing whatever is harming or not helping us. We do not focus on the warning indicators which show us that we are risking our health with our lifestyles.

Being your own bodyguard means having your own back. You know better than anyone how you feel in any given moment. Noticing what influences that and what would make you feel better means you are best placed for the job. Too often we ignore the signs, and it means that we leave it too late and then need to ask for help. Asking for help is not a bad thing at all, it is a good thing to do. Most of us will need some help professionally or informally at some point over a lifetime. With focus you can assess your feelings and see if self-care can help. Then you can decide what else you might need.

The Big question

How well are you looking after you?

The Five Ways to Focus

We can focus our minds on five simple ways to self-care here and this simple technique can be reapplied whenever we need to give ourselves a mini wellbeing check. This can keep us on track to live our best life, giving our minds and our bodies the best chance to thrive.

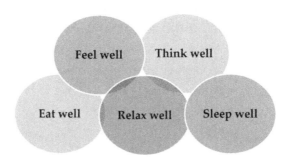

1. **Feel Well**
2. **Think Well**
3. **Eat Well**
4. **Relax well**
5. **Sleep Well**

Way to focus 1: Feel well

How do you know if you feel well? How about a quick body scan? Yes, right now if you are not too busy, that would be great.

The Body Scan

Sitting comfortably in a chair, close your eyes and just imagine a scanner working its way down your body from the top of your head to your feet. Are there any parts that hurt or are injured? How have you looked after that part of you? Does it need your attention or are you hoping it will go away? Are there any parts that used to hurt that are now healed and strong? Notice this too and feel gratitude for the amazing healing machine of your own body. Take a few minutes for this exercise. Then open your eyes again- otherwise you won't be able to read the rest of the book and I would hate for you to miss out.

Insight Questions- Feel Well

1. How do you know you feel well?

2. Can you describe it?

3. What helps you to feel well?

Way to focus 2: Think Well

When we think well, our thoughts are clear and rational. We have the headspace to understand situations, to solve problems and to think ahead without fear or worry, without calamatising or catastrophising. Thinking well is sensing that you have a good emotional balance, letting go of anger that can cause internal pain, and having the energy to do the things you enjoy. Emotional turmoil can be such an energy sapper.

 When we experience the peace of our own minds, we tend to be more emotionally present and engaged with others

We listen better to others when we have our own thoughts in order.

Learning to Think Well

Learning to think well can help your health by emotionally cushioning you from the demands and setbacks of everyday life. Self-care can build resilience in this way to ensure you bounce back more quickly from difficulties. Thinking well is not avoiding the difficulties in life, or not thinking about the tough stuff; it is about emotionally preparing for them and processing them. Building defences and wearing armour does not really protect us from emotions, it just deflects them elsewhere, sometimes onto others.

Avoiding emotional situations by not expressing our feelings can be unhelpful. Most often this means that those feelings do come out but in unexpected ways when you boil over or lose it, sometimes aiming the rant at unsuspecting recipients who just happen to be in the line of fire or love you enough to let you spill your frustration and hurt in their direction, knowing that they are not to blame.

Even people who appear to be cool as cucumbers on the outside may be wrangling with worry or having tumultuous thoughts. When you practice having a focus on thinking well, you will become more aware of what helps or what gets in the way of this. Having a couple of moments to talk yourself down from a sense of escalating panic is a handy little technique to apply. This way of rationalizing thoughts before they become enormous emotions can help you re-centre yourself.

Account for Abundance

An abundance mindset can serve you well and strengthen your resilience, shifting your focus from fear to gratitude and hope.

'Acknowledging the good that you already have in your life is the foundation for all abundance.' -Eckhart Tolle

Practicing the art of abundance can help people be more adjusted to dealing with setbacks by seeing the opportunities. Positive self- talk works wonders. Preparing positive affirmations to recite once you notice your thinking needs a little reset can be a powerful self-care tool to use at any time. Practised daily it can be a key to creating happiness and serenity from cultivating a true sense of all that you are and all that you have.

Insight Questions- Think Well

1. What good thoughts keep you well?

2. What thoughts tend to get in the way?

3. How well do you manage emotions?

Way to focus 3: Eat Well

'The only way to keep your health is to eat what you don't want, drink what you don't like, and do what you'd rather not.' Mark Twain

My guess is that you already know the foods that are good for you and those that are not. The foods we eat can have an enormous effect on our wellbeing and as part of our self-care it is important to have a little check-in and see what you might need to introduce into your diet that will give you the nutrients you need.

Food and drink are not just fuel and should be enjoyed as a way of nourishing and reviving your body and mind. So, maybe take a few moments to think about your meals. Consider how well you are eating and whether you are eating enough good foods. See if you are having the right portion size and having proper meals at regular times. Think about how your intake affects your energy and how you feel about yourself. Try the Goldilocks test for portion control, not too much, not too little but just right. Consider your relationship with food and if you have a positive attitude towards nurturing your body and taking good care of yourself.

Insight Questions- Eat Well

1. How do you feel about what you eat?

2. Do you eat enough healthy foods?

3. Do you limit the amount of unhealthy foods/ drinks that you consume?

Way to focus 4: Relax Well

Relaxation and sleep are very different things. A little relaxation can boost us and help us keep going or can help us recharge our batteries. Too often we let ourselves run out of energy and it is only at the point of exhaustion that we think about relaxing. We can plan to relax in advance when we know we have a demanding day or task ahead. Scheduling a calming walk after a full-on day on Zoom could help forgo the fatigue, or you could book a massage to follow a long journey. Even ten minutes of deep breathing can do wonders for relaxation. Imagine letting your breath be a broom that sweeps away the mental messiness leaving you space to focus on what matters. Allow the little things that don't need your concern to be blown away.

Personally, I think you can't beat a Nana nap. Setting the alarm for twenty minutes in the middle of the day and having a short snooze is a great way to take yourself away from the hubbub of thoughts in your busy brain. Yes, it might take a bit of practice to get in the habit of knowing when this will be helpful to you, and it requires you giving yourself permission to step off the mad merry-go-round for a short time. It is a great treat to self and can sharpen your focus, so you feel reset and ready for anything.

Insight Questions- Relax Well

1. Do you find it easy to relax?

2. What is your best way to relax?

3. When is it important for you to relax?

Way to focus 5: Sleep Well

We make better choices when we are thinking clearly and being well rested is important for clarity of thought. There is a very good reason that sleep deprivation is a tried and tested torture technique because not having enough sleep causes absolute misery and means our bodies and our minds can no longer function at their best. For anyone who has been the parent of a new-born you will know this. For anyone who has had a job where they have had to shuttle back and forth across time zones or work night shifts you know this too.

Not needing sleep has been worn as a badge of honour by some. And there are people who will happily quote that they get by on four hours a night, 4 hours- just like Winston Churchill or Margaret Thatcher did. Arianne Huffington threw doubt on that being something to be proud of. She was brave enough to espouse the idea of sleep being important and suggests we should seek to have seven hours of decent slumber each night.

Refreshed and Recharged

Being your best self does include getting the right amount of sleep for you. 'Getting by' is surviving not thriving and you may need more sleep than you currently have.

FIVE WAYS TO FOCUS

'Sleep is that golden chain that ties health and our bodies together.' -
Thomas Dekker.

If you are going through hormonal changes like the menopause and plagued by insomnia or if a new baby or big work project is keeping you up at night, perhaps it is time to focus on how this is affecting you. Exploring what you can do about this is important before it affects your overall health and wellbeing.

Maybe you have got into some night-time habits that mean you are still on your phone until the wee hours. Blue light from electronic devices stimulates our brains and the recommendation is to switch off two hours before sleep. Many of us use our phones as our alarms so using a power down setting ahead of bedtime and activating the do-not-disturb function is a good way to ensure you can drift off undisturbed each night.

Noticing what you need to have in place to have a blissful, nourishing sleep so you wake refreshed and recharged is important. Preparing well for good sleep makes a difference; it doesn't just happen easily for everyone. A few hours before bed, make a note about things you need to focus on the following day and then turn off the sleep-stealers before settling down to relax before sleeping.

Insight Questions - Sleep Well

1. How well do you sleep?

2. What prevents you sleeping well?

3. What helps?

4. What else could you try?

Well, there we are, we have explored five key aspects of being well. Focus your efforts now on what will make a difference most of all to you.

Action Questions

1. What self-care actions will you take forwards to…?

    a. Feel Well

    b. Think Well

    c. Eat Well

    d. Relax well

    e. Sleep Well

2. When will you put these actions in place?

3. What will help you to be successful in taking these actions?

4. What outcomes are you looking for?

5. What will happen if you take no action?

11. Finding Ways to Focus in order to Flourish

This book has been all about you. When we take note of what is going on for us, we expand our opportunities to grow and learn from our insight. With new perspective we find ways to become our best selves.

I hope that Five Ways to Focus has equipped you with a new set of tools to beat the overwhelm, deal with the distraction, and have the insights about yourself to bring clarity and new perspectives.

Together we have shone the spotlight on what really matters to you, and why, explored what works well for you and what needs to change. We have challenged current thinking and channelled commitments to action. We have adjusted perspective from what is wrong to what is strong and identified what can be even better.

'To learn and not to do is really not to learn. To know and not to do is really not to know.'- Steven Covey

With your new outlook you can embrace what is available to you and look at what has passed and cannot be changed with acceptance. You can see where you are now with kind eyes and look forward to your future encouraged by the knowledge that you have ways to focus on being a happier and fulfilled person. From here, you can cultivate inner peace and move forwards with ease and enthusiasm.

What Now? What Next?

With all this self-knowledge it is important not to slip back into the old ways of being. Before you go, why not...?

1. Consider how well some things are going and congratulate yourself for this.

2. Note your most profound insights and planned actions from each of the five ways.

3. Remind yourself of things which could be better but now you have a plan to get there.

4. Use your new focus to serve those things that need more attention to get things on the up.

5. Treat yourself with kindness; we are all works in progress.

How coaching can help

It may be clearer than ever now that you are at a change point and ready to explore your options and discover what you are really capable of. Or you might see now that you are at boiling point and it is time to dial down the pressure and discover a new way of being that means being your best self, more of the time. If coaching seems like the next step, if you want to explore what has shown up for you here and discover even more ways to get things on the up, you can contact me via my website ontheupconsulting.com. I look forward to hearing from you.

FIVE WAYS TO FOCUS

About the Author

 Julia Wolfendale lives in the North West of England with her two daughters, husband and pesky cat. As an Executive Coach and Founder of On The Up Consulting Ltd, it is her mission to help people be their best selves. Julia's coaching work in organisations is award-winning and she is known for finding fun ways to talk about the tough stuff.

When she is not coaching or training, she is usually having a fun time with soulful people, engaging in sporadic bouts of running, flexing a yoga pose, eating dark chocolate, or conjuring up ideas for future books. Julia is also the author of children's story, <u>The Trouble With Elephants,</u> an uplifting, historical tale about hope and determination.

Twitter @JuliaWolfendale @ontheupbooks

Acknowledgments

Writing a book is a solitary task for the most part, yet I know this book would not have come to be without the support, encouragement, and friendship of significant people in my life.

Having a fabulous husband and lovely daughters has helped me know what really matters. You are loved, thank you for the joy you bring.

Thank you to my marvellous mum and dad for your love and belief in me. I am fortunate to have wonderful friends, soulful people who are always ready to listen and make me smile, especially, Emma, Fiona, Jo, Claire, Kate, Gary and Pam.

Huge thanks to Louise Bond, my skilful editor for her insightful recommendations, scrupulous attention to detail and endless patience (louisebondfreelancewriter.co.uk). Toby Potter, the talented designer of the front cover artwork, thank you so much for your creativity and versatility, I know I am always in good hands when I come to you with a design project.

And finally, to my clients, thank you for trusting me to work with you and help you get where you want to be.

Also by Julia Wolfendale:

Novels

The Trouble with Elephants

Thank you for purchasing this book. If you have found it useful please leave a review at amazon.co.uk.

Follow the author

Resources

You can find additional resources including the guided visualisation, template worksheet to record your answers to the questions in this book and a life audit at,

https://www.ontheupconsulting.com/finding-ways-to-focus/

If you would like to receive updates on books, book signings, events, courses and coaching services you can subscribe at

www.ontheupconsulting.com

Try out the Five Ways to Focus online course on Udemy.com
https://www.udemy.com/course/five-ways-to-focus-a-self-led-coaching-programme/

References and Further Reading

Canfield, J., & Switzer, J. 2005. *The Success Principles: How to get from where you are to where you want to be.* Harper Collins.

Wolfendale, J. 2020. *Five Ways to Focus: A Self-Led Coaching Programme,* On the Up Consulting Ltd available on Udemy.com, https://www.udemy.com/course/five-ways-to-focus-a-self-led-coaching-programme/learn/lecture/23285512#content

Ofcom. 2018. *A Decade of Digital Dependency* https://www.ofcom.org.uk/about-ofcom/latest/features-and-news/decade-of-digital-dependency

Kahneman, D. 2015. *Thinking, Fast and Slow.* New York: Farrar, Straus and Giroux.

Royal Society of Public Health. 2017. *#StatusofMind.* The Young Health Movement. London: RSPH https://www.rsph.org.uk/static/uploaded/d125b2 7c-0b62-41c5-a2c0155a8887cd01.pdf

Time Magazine. 2017. New York https://time.com/4793331/instagram-social-media-mental-health/

David, S. 2018. *The gift and power of emotional courage.*https://www.youtube.com/watch?v=ND Q1Mi5I4rg

Bridges. J. 2004. *Making Sense of Life's Changes.* Da Capo Press.

Redfield, J. 1993. *The celestine prophecy: An adventure.* Warner Books.

Maple, J. 2018. *The pocket book of mindfulness: Live in the moment and reduce stress.* Arcturus Ltd.

Cherry, K. Updated on July 30, 2021. *How Multitasking Affects Productivity and Brain Health,* https://www.verywellmind.com/what-is-attention-2795009

Barrett, A. June 2020. *Return to work: does COVID-19 mark the end of the office?* Science Focus.https://www.sciencefocus.com/news/return-to-work-does-covid-19-mark-the-end-of-the-office/

Office for National Statistics.2021, *Business and individual attitudes towards the future of homeworking, UK: April to May 2021.* London.

https://www.ons.gov.uk/employmentandlabourmarket/peopleinwork/employmentandemployeetypes/articles/businessandindividualattitudestowardsthefutureofhomeworkinguk/apriltomay2021

Statista Research Department. May 11 2021.

Number of freelancers in the U.S. 2017-2028.

https://www.statista.com/statistics/921593/gig-economy-number-of-freelancers-us/

World Health Organisation. 2011. *Global Status Report on Noncommunicable Diseases 2010.* Geneva, Switzerland: World Health Organization. https://apps.who.int/iris/bitstream/handle/10665/44579/9789240686458_eng.pdf;sequence=1

Good Work Index report. June 2020. *Work making our wellbeing worse – even before COVID-19 crisis started, CIPD releases latest.* https://www.cipd.co.uk/about/media/press/good-word-index-2020#gref

Covey, S. R. 1989. *The seven habits of highly effective people: Restoring the character ethic*. New York: Simon and Schuster.

Young, E. 2016. *Sane*. London: Yellow Kite.

Snyder, C. 2002. *Hope Theory: rainbows in the mind*. Psychological Inquiry. 13: 249-275

Frankl, V. E., Pisano, H., Lasch, I., Kushner, H. S., & Winslade, W. J. 2014. *Man's search for meaning.*

Simply Psychology. 29 December 2020 *Maslow's Hierarchy of Needs.* Archived from the original on 8 November 2018. Retrieved 8 November 2018.

Confederation of British Industry. 2021. *Gender Pay Gap Report* https://www.cbi.org.uk/media/6912/gender-pay-gap-report-2021.pdf

Killingworth, M. January 26, 2021 *Experienced well-being rises with income, even above $75,000 per year.* PNAS 118 (4):https://doi.org/10.1073/pnas2016976118

Samuel J., June 2019. *With Social Media, Everyone's A Celebrity.* JSTOR https://daily.jstor.org/with-social-media-everyones-a-celebrity/

Krznaric, R. 2013. *How to find fulfilling work.* Picador.

Seligman. M, Steen,T, Peterson, C. 2005. *Positive Psychology Progress Empirical Validation of Interventions.* https://soulsweet.de/wp-content/uploads/2017/05/Seligman-Tracy.pdf

Peale, N. V. 1952. *The power of positive thinking.* New York: Prentice-Hall

Tolle, E. 1999. *The power of now: A guide to spiritual enlightenment.* Novato: California.

Chopra, D. 2010. *The ultimate happiness prescription: 7 keys to joy and enlightenment.* London: Rider.

Andrade, E.A., Ariely, D. *'The enduring impact of transient emotions on decision making' Organizational Behavior and Human Decision*

Processes.May 2009, Volume 109, Issue 1, ,
Pages 1-8,
https://www.sciencedirect.com/science/article/abs/pii/S0749597809000211

West, M. 2021. *What is the fight, flight, or freeze response?* Medical News Today accessed on September 20 2021.
https://www.medicalnewstoday.com/articles/fight-flight-or-freeze-response#freeze

Fry, A.. 2020. *'Napping'. Sleep Foundation.*
.https://www.sleepfoundation.org/sleep-hygiene/napping

Huffington, A. 2016. *The Sleep Revolution.* Penguin Random House.

Printed in Great Britain
by Amazon

28814898R00110